D0222502

EXERCISES

TO ACCOMPANY

THE RINEHART HANDBOOK FOR WRITERS
Fourth Edition

Bonnie Carter
Craig Skates

formerly of
The University of Southern Mississippi

Harcourt Brace College Publishers

Fort Worth   Philadelphia   San Diego   New York   Orlando   Austin   San Antonio
Toronto   Montreal   London   Sydney   Tokyo

Copyright © 1996 by Holt, Rinehart and Winston, Inc.

All rights reserved. No part of this publication may be reproduced or
transmitted in any form or by any means, electronic or mechanical,
including photocopy, recording, or any information storage and retrieval
system, without permission in writing from the publisher.

Requests for permission to make copies of any part of the work should be
mailed to: Permissions Department, Harcourt Brace & Company, 6277
Sea Harbor drive, Orlando, Florida 32887-6777.

Some material in this work previously appeared in *The Rinehart
Handbook for Writers*, Third Edition, copyright © 1993, 1990, 1988 by
Holt, Rinehart and Winston, Inc. All rights reserved.

Address for Editorial Correspondence: Harcourt Brace College Publishers,
301 Commerce Street, Suite 3700, Fort Worth, TX 76102.

Address for Orders:
Harcourt Brace & Company, 6277 Sea Harbor Drive, Orlando, Florida
32887-6777, 1-800-782-4479 or 1-800-435-0001 (in Florida).

Printed in the United States of America

ISBN: 0-15-503134-1

5 6 7 8 9 0 1 2 3 4 066 0 9 8 7 6 5 4 3 2 1

CONTENTS

PART II
Structural and
Grammatical Problems   37

PART III
Punctuation and Mechanics   79

PART IV
Style   119

PART I

A Review of
the Basics

Chapter 1

Nouns

1a Exercise 1

For each common noun listed, give a corresponding proper noun.

EXAMPLE: building   Pentagon

1. political party
2. religion
3. family member
4. governmental body
5. historical figure
6. holiday
7. city
8. river
9. club
10. war

1a–1b Exercise 2

Find the nouns, both common and proper, in the following sentences. Identify each as singular or plural.

1. The traditional gift for a sixtieth wedding anniversary is a diamond.
2. The Mohave Desert has unusual varieties of cacti.
3. Vitamin D, important for bone development, is derived from sunlight.
4. Bristlecone pines, which grow in the White Mountains of California, are thought to be the oldest trees in the world.
5. The ecology of the lake has been upset.
6. Reindeer are capable of running thirty miles an hour.

1b Exercise 3

Give the plural form (or forms) for each singular noun listed. If you have any doubt about a correct form, consult a dictionary.

1. shrimp
2. touchdown
3. wolf
4. index
5. day
6. candy
7. runner-up
8. bypass
9. passerby
10. leave of absence
11. crisis
12. poet laureate
13. antenna
14. index
15. memo

1c Exercise 4

Form a possessive from each of the following phrases.

1. the constitution of Texas
2. the wishes of the alumni
3. absence of five months
4. food for the three cats
5. the plot of the novel

Chapter 2

PRONOUNS

2a Exercise 1

Identify the personal pronouns in the following passage.

Guy Fawkes felt that his Catholic countrymen were being oppressed in seventeenth-century England. He said, "We are being treated as though we were dogs—verminous dogs." A group of Catholics wanted to act on Fawkes's recommendation: "Let us strike at the source where they make the laws." The conspirators decided to blow up the House of Lords by digging a tunnel and filling it with gunpowder. Before the fuse could be lit, the plot was discovered, and Fawkes himself was seized and executed. Strangely enough, he has been immortalized in a Mother Goose rhyme:

Please remember
The fifth of November,
      Gunpowder treason and plot.

I see no reason
Why gunpowder treason
      Should ever be forgot.

2b Exercise 2

Identify the demonstrative pronouns in the following passage.

In 1938, the citizens of Grovers Mill, New Jersey, thought they were being invaded by Martians. This was the year of the radio broadcast of

"The War of the Worlds." Those who heard the program panicked. They ran into the streets and tied up traffic. Those who have never heard the show cannot imagine the impact of the dramatization with its realistic "news flashes." That dramatization brought to life the Martians with "saliva dripping from . . . rimless lips" invading Grovers Mill. Details like these even caused one farmer to shoot at the water tower, mistaking it for the aliens' spacecraft.

2c Exercise 3

Identify the relative pronouns in the following passage.

An enjoyable hobby that does not involve any talent or expense is collecting what I call "sign bloopers." The term refers to any sign that is misleading or unintentionally humorous. For example, here are two from my own collection:

> Sign on door of high school: "Please use other door. This door is broke."

> Sign in lounge: "We reserve the right to refuse service to everyone."

Anyone who has a notebook and pencil can start a collection. Furthermore, anyone whose mind is alert to the written word can accumulate quite a few prized items in a short while. Most bloopers appear in hand-lettered signs, which are common in family-owned businesses and places where employees want to give temporary instructions. Two more bloopers that I have collected can illustrate.

> Sign in diner: "No chicks please."

> Sign in tax collector's office: "Motor vehicles use other line."

2d–2e Exercise 4

Identify the indefinite and interrogative pronouns in the following passage.

Horse-racing records aren't often broken; in fact, few have been broken in fifteen years. Who knows why? Some think that the trainers want to win races, not break records. Others think that the best horses now go into breeding before they reach their full speed. Still others believe that horses cannot run faster than they run now. What is the reason? In the opinion of many, the training methods are outdated. Until someone comes up with effective new methods, everything around the racetrack will probably stay the same.

2a–2e Exercise 5

Locate the pronouns in the following passage and identify their types as personal, demonstrative, relative, interrogative, or indefinite.

Who gives us the best advice about nutrition? The advice we get is often contradictory and leaves us thoroughly confused. For example, some advisors condone vitamin supplements; others advise against them. According to some authorities, meat is nutritionally indispensable. However, many studies suggest that it contributes to coronary problems and cancer. Nutritional controversies also rage over salt, sugar, fiber, and fat. These substances are usually recommended for our diets, but in different quantities—sometimes liberal, sometimes limited. When the authorities don't agree, what are we to do? We can only await new studies that may provide answers.

Chapter 3

ADJECTIVES AND ADVERBS

3a Exercise 1

Insert adjectives to modify the nouns in the following sentences.

1. Next to the sandwich was a pile of fries.
2. The model wore a skirt, a sweater, and cowboy boots.
3. The worms in the can wiggled in moss.
4. The batter yelled at the umpire and the fans.
5. Around the castle was a moat.
6. The interviewer's attitude grated on my nerves.
7. His library was filled with maps.
8. Our bonfire shed a light on the beach.
9. A stairway let to a balcony.
10. The job led me to consider a change.

3b Exercise 2

Write sentences containing the following types of adverbs.

1. an adverb made by adding -*ly* to an adjective
2. an adverb made with the suffix -*ward*
3. a qualifier modifying an adverb
4. a qualifier modifying an adjective
5. an adverb that can also be a preposition

3a–3b Exercise 3

Identify the modifiers in the following sentences as adjectives or adverbs.

1. The value of the new stock jumped dramatically.
2. The old town had a rather efficient sawmill; nevertheless, the economy was distressed.
3. The company now reluctantly accepts full responsibility.
4. Abruptly, the local newspaper quit printing the controversial cartoon.
5. The white Persian kittens were extremely fat.
6. The painting graphically portrayed the cruel war.
7. Sometimes anti-inflammatory drugs can permanently damage an athlete.
8. The obviously professional thieves carried out a lucrative theft.
9. The pedantic professors discussed their views on genetic engineering.
10. The contributions of Edward R. Murrow are very important to contemporary journalism.

3c Exercise 4

In each sentence, use the appropriate form of the adjective or adverb shown in parentheses.

1. Electric cars ran (fast) than steam cars.
2. Of all those who spoke, the first candidate gave the (weak) speech.
3. The Egyptian exhibit was (fascinating) than any other.
4. Shaw's play *Pygmalion* was transformed into *My Fair Lady,* one of the (popular) musicals of all time.
5. The (small) species of shark grows to no longer than six inches.
6. Her backhand was (good) than anyone else's on the team.
7. Last night we saw the (bad) movie of the year.
8. My partner played her cards (expertly) than I.
9. The language with the (large) vocabulary is English.
10. Your apartment is (near) campus than mine.

Chapter 4

VERBS AND VERB PHRASES

4a Exercise 1

Fill in the following chart.

	BASE	-s FORM	PAST FORM	PAST PARTICIPLE	PRESENT PARTICIPLE
EX.	lift	lifts	lifted	lifted	lifting
1.	forbid				
2.	spin				
3.	shred				
4.	burn				
5.	lead				
6.	beat				
7.	burst				
8.	creep				

4a Exercise 2

Supply the verbs called for in the parentheses.

1. The sea gull (past of *dive*) into the water.
2. Fate has (past participle of *deal*) him a cruel blow.
3. The camper (past of *lie*) on the cold ground all night.
4. The consumer (-s form of *pay*) the price for advertisements.
5. The stations are (present participle of *get*) interference.
6. The stock has (past participle of *be*) listed in the exchange for the past year.
7. The troops (past of *flee*) the battlefield.
8. He (-s form of *try*) to play halfback.

9. The project has (past participle of *have*) a number of setbacks.
10. The map will (base form of *show*) you the shortest route.

4b Exercise 3

Rewrite the following sentences, changing the verbs in order to add the auxiliaries indicated.

EXAMPLE: We finished the work before dark. (must) → we <u>must finish</u> the work before dark.

1. Their shop sells homemade quilts. (will)
2. The general led a successful coup. (can)
3. The chefs prepare an excellent chocolate mousse. (have)
4. The museum has sold the painting. (may)
5. The newspaper reported the murder. (did)
6. He played the stock market. (should)
7. The hotel made a profit. (has)
8. A conference on pollution takes place in August. (is)
9. We will leave by Friday. (have)
10. A library staff has assembled the collection. (been)

4b Exercise 4

Write sentences containing verb phrases in the combinations of auxiliaries and main verbs listed.

EXAMPLE: modal auxiliary + *have* auxiliary + past participle of *see* → You <u>should have seen</u> the game last night.

1. modal auxiliary + base form of *type*
2. *have* auxiliary + past participle of *go*
3. *be* auxiliary + present participle of *live*
4. modal auxiliary + *be* auxiliary + present participle of *sleep*
5. modal auxiliary + *have* auxiliary + past participle of *know*
6. *do* auxiliary + base form of *deny*
7. *have* auxiliary + *be* auxiliary + present participle of *read*
8. modal auxiliary + *have* auxiliary + *be* auxiliary + past participle of *see*

4c Exercise 5

Identify the tense of each verb and verb phrase in the following sentences.

1. They have planned the museum's textile exhibit carefully.
2. He collected all Glenn Gould's recordings of Bach.
3. The freighter travels down the Mississippi to New Orleans every spring.
4. Trisodium phosphate will remove grease and heavy stains.
5. He had hoped for one victory on the PGA tour.
6. The veterinarian now does dental work on dogs.
7. The erosion will have caused an irreversible problem by next year.
8. In Goethe's drama, Faust sold his soul to Mephistopheles.
9. He had not applied for the job before the deadline.
10. The dancers have practiced pirouettes for two hours.

4c Exercise 6

Write a sentence using each verb in the tense indicated. Include enough detail in each sentence so that the tense seems appropriate.

In other words, avoid writing sentences such as *I see, I ran, I will tell you,* and the like.

EXAMPLE: Past perfect tense of *leave*
            The train <u>had left</u> a half hour before I reached the station.

1. present tense of *clean*
2. past tense of *ride*
3. future tense of *type*
4. present perfect tense of *select*
5. past perfect tense of *hope*
6. future perfect tense of *complete*

4d Exercise 7

In the following sentences, identify the tense of each progressive verb form.

1. The agency is now considering candidates for director.
2. Red wines from France's Phone region were selling well.

3. After the new guidelines are established, the commission will be rating movies on a scale of one to four.
4. Before the recession, the company had been growing rapidly.
5. In May the factory will have been using robots for six months.
6. Psychics have been predicting earthquakes in Tennessee.
7. Experts are restoring the building to its original state.
8. The hurricane had been moving toward Texas when it suddenly reversed its course.
9. At sunrise the barges were crossing the river.
10. The city has been issuing bonds for school construction for the past ten years.

4a–4d Exercise 8

Write sentences using each of the following verb forms. Include enough detail so that readers can see why each verb is appropriate to its sentence.

EXAMPLE: <u>had given</u>
<u>I had given</u> the painting away before I found out how valuable it was.

1. catch
2. burns
3. is fighting
4. rode
5. had hurt
6. was drawing
7. has been selling
8. were sleeping
9. had been drinking
10. will learn

4e Exercise 9

Identify the verbs in the following sentences as active or passive.

1. The tour leader was lecturing the group in the Library of Congress.
2. The proposition was explained to the marketing representatives.
3. The radio advertisement is not attracting buyers.
4. Airlines offer reduced fares to people over sixty-five.
5. The bank has notified the company by telephone.
6. The essays in the collection are all written by scientists.
7. Clam chowder is always served on Friday.
8. The courier must deliver the package by five o'clock.

4e   Exercise 10

Change the following passive-voice sentences to active.

EXAMPLE: The dents in the car were made by hailstones. → Hailstones made the dents in the car.

1. Nutritional problems are sometimes overlooked by doctors.
2. Few memberships have been accepted by the club.
3. In *The Pride of the Yankees,* Lou Gehrig was played by Gary Cooper.
4. Gas production has been hampered by control laws.
5. The hillsides were blanketed with wild flowers.

4e Exercise 11

Change the following active voice sentences to passive and delete the resulting *by* phrase.

EXAMPLE: The citizens elect a president every four years. → A president is elected every four years.

1. Witnesses saw the suspect driving a red convertible.
2. The school named her Outstanding Teacher of the Year.
3. You can purchase tickets two weeks in advance.
4. The company publishes the book only in paperback.
5. People expect doctors to be infallible.

4f Exercise 12

Determine whether the mood of each underlined verb is indicative, imperative, or subjunctive.

1. Stalin <u>planned</u> to liquidate some of his political associates.
2. The constitution requires that a majority <u>be</u> present to vote.
3. To keep your terrarium from souring, <u>add</u> broken charcoal.
4. The dreadful extravaganza <u>will cost</u> about ten million.
5. Two free throws <u>were made</u> in the final minute.   .
6. <u>Describe</u> what you see in the ink blots.

7. Most Asian countries insist that a visitor <u>receive</u> cholera injections before entry.
8. If I <u>were</u> in Italy during August, I would avoid Venice.
9. The sprinklers <u>have been running</u> all weekend.
10. It is imperative that she have privacy.

Chapter 5

VERBALS AND VERBAL PHRASES

5a Exercise 1

Combine the following pairs of sentences by changing the second sentence in each pair to an infinitive phrase.

EXAMPLE: Listen to your voice on a tape recording. You can find out how you sound to other people. → To find out how you sound to other people, listen to your voice on a tape recording.

1. The plant must install equipment. The equipment must limit the pollutants emitted.
2. The jockey uses a crop. The crop gives a horse special signals.
3. Galileo designed the sector. The sector aids draftsmen.
4. At night the hippopotamus leaves the water. At night the hippopotamus feeds on land.
5. Packwood and Brinson Inc. has been hired. Packwood and Brinson Inc. will design the museum.
6. The United States uses artificial satellites. The satellites obtain weather information.
7. The tourists visited Argentina. The tourists will see Buenos Aires.
8. Hannibal's military genius helped him. Hannibal defeated armies much larger than his.
9. The Argonauts sailed with Jason. The Argonauts searched for the Golden Fleece.
10. The scientists use a particle accelerator. The scientists study atomic particles such as neutrinos.

5b Exercise 2

Combine each pair of sentences by changing the second to a participial phrase. Position the participle carefully so that it clearly refers to the word it modifies.

EXAMPLE: Vivaldi's works included instrumental compositions and operas. Vivaldi's works were admired by Bach. →
<u>Admired by Bach</u>, Vivaldi's works included instrumental compositions and operas.

1. The book describes current medical discoveries. The discoveries are revolutionizing cancer treatment.
2. The people filled the street in front of the Capitol. The people were protesting the law.
3. The tour goes to forty destinations. The destinations include ten stops in China.
4. We purchased a charcoal grill. The charcoal grill was designed for a commercial restaurant.
5. The first European explorers found that many Indian tribes farmed the land. European explorers arrived in South America.
6. Authorities continued searching for three members of a family. The family was missing after a twister ripped apart their house.
7. At one time Thebes was the most powerful city-state in all Greece. Thebes supposedly was founded by Cadmus.
8. Tutankhamen's tomb contained a coffin of solid gold. The coffin is now located in the Cairo Museum.

5c Exercise 3

Identify the gerunds and gerund phrases in the following sentences.

1. By marrying a Persian princess, Alexander the Great encouraged intermarriage.
2. Looking too far into the future can be frightening.
3. A typewriter's bell prevents typing past the right margin.
4. *All the King's Men* describes the making of a powerful Southern politician.
5. Amoebas reproduce by fission, or splitting apart.
6. Many experts consider jogging the best aerobic exercise.
7. A current fad among amateur photographers is developing film.

8. Fred Astaire gave dancing an athletic grace.
9. Balancing a job and school can take careful planning.
10. Sunlight, temperature, precipitation, soil condition, plants, and animals—all these elements go into forming a "natural community."

5d Exercise 4

Which of the following sentences contain absolute phrases?

1. Attaching itself to a shark, the remora gets both transportation and protection.
2. The weather being cool and dry, they suggested an old-fashioned hayride.
3. To make a long story short, the only fish we caught swam into the boat when it capsized.
4. Strictly speaking, the tomato is not a vegetable.
5. Suddenly we saw the dog, his hackles raised and his teeth bared for attack.
6. To escape the noise of the dormitory, I began studying in the library.
7. Soaring through the clouds, the little plane looked much like a graceful seagull.
8. We searched for the location of the town, the map spread out before us.
9. I awoke slowly, my head pounding, my eyes burning with fever.
10. To conclude, the program cannot survive without federal funds.

5a–5d Exercise 5

Find the verbal phrases in the following sentences. Classify each as an infinitive, participle, gerund, or absolute phrase.

1. We are grateful to the Olympic athletes for representing our country so well.
2. The book includes all maps relating to the Lewis and Clark expedition.
3. To write a computer program takes skill and patience.
4. Heads nodding and eyelids drooping, the students struggled to follow the boring lecture.

5. The three-barred cross, also known as the Russian cross, is a symbol of the Russian Orthodox Church.
6. Cargo fits in containers shaped to conform to the airplane's interior.
7. Three reporters, camped out on the mayor's front lawn, were evicted by the police.
8. A peninsula jutting out from the northwest corner of France, Brittany was once an independent state.
9. This combination of chemicals has the potential to explode.
10. Cheating on taxes has become a serious problem.
11. Soaring in ascending circles, the eagle rose higher and higher.
12. Completed last year, the excavation uncovered a Roman street.

5a–5d Exercise 6

Write sentences containing the following verbal phrases.

1. an infinitive phrase
2. a gerund phrase
3. two participle phrases
4. an absolute phrase
5. an infinitive phrase and a participle phrase

Chapter 6

FUNCTION WORDS

6a Exercise 1

Identify the prepositional phrases in the following sentences.

1. Because of the music, this advertisement about soft drinks appeals to young people.
2. In the nineteenth century, American literature broke away from British tradition.
3. We were happy about their arrival and ecstatic over their departure.
4. For thousands of years, monks have used chant as a part of their sacred liturgy.
5. In the mornings before ten will be convenient.

6b (1) Exercise 2

Use coordinating conjunctions to combine the pairs of sentences. Join either words, phrases, or clauses.

1. You can work out on the Nautilus machines. On the other hand, you can work out on the free weights.
2. Politicians came to the meeting in Chicago. Financiers came to the meeting in Chicago.
3. There are nearly fifty legal grounds for divorce. The majority of American suits are filed for cruelty.
4. Alec Guinness appeared in *The Bridge on the River Kwai.* He appeared in *Lawrence of Arabia.*
5. The sky is crystal clear. The moon is almost full.

6b (3) Exercise 3

Combine the pairs of sentences by using subordinating conjunctions.

EXAMPLE: I did not pay my bill for two months. So the phone company disconnected my telephone. → The phone company disconnected my telephone because I did not pay my bill for two months.

1. The plane descended. We saw the Washington Monument.
2. Prehistoric humans did no cultivating. They were forced into nomadic life.
3. Father grew older. He became less and less able to farm without help.
4. I was only twelve. But I could fly a P51 Mustang.
5. Their favorite restaurant was an outdoor cafe. They had both worked there ten years before.

6b (4) Exercise 4

Use a comparative conjunction and a clause to specify degree in each of the following sentences.

EXAMPLE

ORIGINAL: The area is subject to flooding. (How subject is it to flooding?)

REVISED: The area is so subject to flooding that no one should build a house there.

1. The drink was bitter. (How bitter was it?)
2. They are close friends. (How close are they?)
3. The picnic was enjoyable. The dance was enjoyable. (Which one was more enjoyable?)
4. The skater performed poorly. (How poorly did she perform?)
5. This racetrack is fast. (How fast is it?)

6a–6b Exercise 5

Use conjunctions to combine the sets of sentences. You can choose coordinating, correlative, subordinating, or comparative conjunctions— whichever is appropriate. Identify each you choose.

EXAMPLE

ORIGINAL: The computer program is efficient. It makes editing simpler. It eliminates retyping.

COMBINED: The computer program is efficient because it makes editing simpler and eliminates retyping.

1. The presidential seal shows the American eagle clutching arrows in one talon. The eagle is clutching an olive branch in the other.
2. Nuclear plants produce electricity without air pollution. Nuclear fission has several disadvantages.
3. Bob Marley died in 1981. He is considered the creator of the best Jamaican reggae music.
4. The moon's revolution is irregular. The irregular revolution is due to the fact that its orbit is elliptical.
5. The camera is versatile. The camera comes with a telephoto lens. It also comes with a wide-angle lens.
6. The little fishing village becomes populated in the summer. It is populated like a bustling city.
7. *Tropic of Cancer* was published. Then Henry Miller became a famous figure. He also became a controversial figure.
8. This organism flourishes in fresh water. It also flourishes in brackish water.
9. The street was hot. It burned my feet through my shoes.
10. Plants do not live alone. Animals do not live alone.

6c Exercise 6

Identify the determiners in the following sentences.

1. Our instructor sent his first story to *Harper's*.
2. December's weather has ruined the fruit crops.
3. Every spring, a heavy rain causes floods in that section of town.
4. Which kinds of cars will people buy this year?
5. The three projects helped eliminate the downtown traffic snarl.
6. Only an inadequate bank account kept him from a life of luxury.

6d Exercise 7

In the following passage, indicate whether each *there* is used as an expletive or an adverb. Also, indicate whether each *it* is used as an expletive or a pronoun.

There are two effective aids to kicking the cigarette habit. First, it helps to motivate yourself by thinking of all the bad effects of smoking—such as wrinkles, coughs, expense, and diseases. You can even tape the list to your bathroom mirror. There you will see it every morning when shaving or putting on makeup. Second, it is advisable to avoid environments like bars and coffeehouses, environments that tempt people to smoke.

Chapter 7

CLAUSES AND SENTENCES

7a (1)–7a (2) Exercise 1

In the following sentences, determine which verbs are intransitive and which are transitive. If you have trouble, use the passive-voice conversion to identify direct objects.

1. The mayor favors higher taxes.
2. Classes begin on September 1.
3. As usual, bad news traveled fast.
4. The Coast Guard rescued the couple after a three-day search.
5. Lightning flashed ominously in the western sky.
6. The author typed her entire 700-page manuscript on a manual typewriter.
7. I bathe and groom both dogs once a week.
8. The disagreement progressed quickly to a shouting match.

7a (2) Exercise 2

Determine which of the following sentences contain indirect objects and which contain object complements. You can identify an indirect object by using the prepositional phrase conversion; you can identify the object complements by using the equation test.

1. Our company awarded the investors a dividend.
2. The city council declared the water unsafe.
3. Bad weather makes my dog nervous.
4. Critics called the play "a sleazy joke."
5. Sing me the lyrics one more time.
6. The old man built the children a carousel.
7. She considered Elizabeth I her role model.
8. After much delay, they offered me the position.

7a (3) Exercise 3

All the following sentences contain linking verbs and subject complements. Identify each verb and determine whether its complement is an adjective, a noun, a possessive, or an adverb.

1. Gradually, I grew weary of his jealousy.
2. The stew tastes bitter.
3. This project has been a disaster.
4. Your umbrella was in the hall closet.
5. For most of us, medical school seemed an endurance test.
6. He remained optimistic in spite of any setbacks.
7. At her father's death, the estate became hers.
8. The best time for the reunion would be July 4th.
9. That pen on your desk is mine.
10. Without my cats, I felt very lonely.

7a Exercise 4

Match the sentences with the patterns listed. All the linking-verb patterns are combined under pattern (e).

(A)   Subject + Intransitive Verb
(B)   Subject + Transitive Verb + Direct Object
(C)   Subject + Transitive Verb + Indirect Object + Direct Object
(D)   Subject + Transitive Verb + Direct Object + Object Complement
(E)   Subject + Linking Verb + Subject Complement

1. The door locks automatically.
2. The Internal Revenue office is downstairs.
3. For America's National symbol, Benjamin Franklin proposed the turkey.
4. The Interior Department has declared the peregrine falcon an endangered species.
5. The refrigerator is one of the biggest users of energy in the home.
6. A ranger showed us the best camp sites.
7. Crying can relieve stress by adjusting body chemistry.
8. My house guests stayed for two weeks.
9. Fresh herbs taste better than the dried variety.
10. The home computer has made financial planning easier.

7a Exercise 5

Match the sentences with the patterns listed. Each linking-verb pattern is listed individually.

(A)   Subject + Intransitive Verb
(B)   Subject + Transitive Verb + Direct Object
(C)   Subject + Transitive Verb + Indirect Object + Direct Object
(D)   Subject + Transitive Verb + Direct Object + Object Complement
(E)   Subject + Linking Verb + Adjective Complement
(F)   Subject + Linking Verb + Noun Or Pronoun Complement
(G)   Subject + Linking Verb + Possessive Complement
(H)   Subject + Linking Verb + Adverb Complement

1.   Weight loss became an obsession to Marsha.
2.   The asparagus seems unsuited to gardens in south Florida.
3.   Every year, the Academy of Television Arts and Sciences awards the best dramatic series an Emmy.
4.   Copyrights now last for the life of an author plus fifty years.
5.   The lot east of this building is the city's.
6.   She told us the history of leather making.
7.   Your taxi will be in front of the hotel.
8.   In 1846, Thoreau spent one night in jail.
9.   Edison called his research laboratory at Menlo Park an "invention factory."
10.   Vanilla seems the most popular ice-cream flavor in this area.
11.   Leaf-cutter ants can strip a tree bare in a day.
12.   American industry can learn from the success of the Japanese.

7c (1) Exercise 6

Combine the following pairs of sentences by making the second one an adverb clause that shows the meaning indicated in the parentheses.

EXAMPLE: The students at Lincoln High School were in seventh-period classes. The fire alarm went off. (time) → The students at Lincoln High were in seventh-period classes when the fire alarm went off.

1.   This state judges criminals insane. They cannot distinguish right from wrong. (condition)

2. Wegener formally proposed the theory of continental drift in
   1912. Others had suggested the idea as early as 1629. (contrast)
3. Dante's poetry helped establish the common language of Italy.
   Chaucer's writings helped establish English. (manner)
4. The Allies kept the plans for the invasion of Normandy a secret.
   They could deceive the Germans about the true landing site.
   (purpose)
5. The archer was accurate. Every arrow hit the gold center.
   (comparison)
6. In the familiar version, Little Red Riding Hood escapes the wolf.
   In the original version, she does not. (contrast)
7. I used to catch colds every winter. I began taking massive doses
   of vitamin C. (time)
8. Snakes weren't a real worry at the campsite. Snakes are fairly
   sluggish in the dry season. (cause)

7c (2) Exercise 7

Combine each pair of sentences by converting the second sentence of
the pair to an adjective clause.

EXAMPLE: Destructive waves are caused by undersea earthquakes
              or hurricanes. The waves sweep in from the ocean. →
              Destructive waves that sweep in from the ocean are
              caused by undersea earthquakes or hurricanes.

1. The hotel was designed for the very rich. The very rich can afford
   unlimited luxuries.
2. During a thunderstorm, you should avoid dangerous locations.
   Dangerous locations are significantly higher than their
   surroundings.
3. The trilogy by Tolkien tells of a ring. The ring's wearer can control
   the world.
4. The computer has a graphics index. The graphics index will file
   and retrieve pictures.
5. Goya's "black paintings" are painted directly on the walls of his
   house. Goya's "black paintings" depict scenes nightmarish and
   grotesque.
6. On September 2, 1945, World War II ended. On September 2,
   1945, the Japanese signed the "instrument of surrender."

7. A Frisbee is named for the Frisbie Bakery. At the Frisbie Bakery, pie tins resembling the plastic disk were used.
8. Orthodox physicians drove Dr. Mesmer from practice in Vienna. Dr. Mesmer developed hypnotism.

7c (3) Exercise 8

In the following sentences, identify each noun clause and its function.

1. What made *The Bridge on the River Kwai* an interesting film was its complex characters with both good and bad traits.
2. Scientists believe there may be millions of insects not yet classified.
3. It is not clear when the composer will finish the music for the new ballet.
4. The new supervisor will be whoever has the best sales record.
5. What interested me most was the exhibition on the history of flight.
6. A part of the legend of Hercules is that under Hera's jealous influence, Hercules killed his wife and children.
7. The British scientists discovered that Piltdown man's skull had the jawbone of a modern ape.
8. From the information in the book, we can draw conclusions about what the early settlers thought.

7d Exercise 9

Identify the elliptical clauses in the following sentences, and supply the missing words in each.

EXAMPLE: I bought the camera while visiting Japan.
            I bought the camera while [I was] visiting Japan.

1. Perseus was given a brass shield as bright as a mirror.
2. Fluorescent lights give more light at a lower energy cost than incandescent bulbs with the same wattage.
3. Some stars burn their hydrogen fuel so fast they explode as supernovas.
4. While analyzing the data on the printout, the astronomers discovered the existence of background radiation.
5. Courtney played with seven different baseball leagues; Chiti, with four.

7a–7c Exercise 10

In the following sentences, underline the independent clauses once and the dependent clauses twice.   Indicate whether the dependent clauses are functioning as nouns, adjectives, or adverbs.

   1. The principal river in the United States is the Mississippi, whose chief literary interpreter was Mark Twain.
   2. Robots are now being installed in the factory, where they can make almost any manufactured product.
   3. They argued over whether they should go to the beach or to the mountains.
   4. One study estimated that illiteracy costs the United States approximately $500 billion a year.
   5. Woodrow Wilson suffered a stroke just as he was striving to popularize his ideas for a League of Nations.
   6. Once people are in a hypnotic trance, they can focus their attention on one thing and ignore distractions.
   7. Some abbreviations that are acceptable in technical reports may not be appropriate in formal essays.
   8. In order that his son could win bicycle races, Dunlop developed the pneumatic tire.
   9. The fight ended as abruptly as it had begun.
   10. Although Dracula died with a stake through his heart in the first film, the monster has reappeared in many sequels.
   11. *The New Yorker,* which was founded in 1925, was first edited by Harold Ross.
   12. It is likely that a raccoon raided the kitchen.

7e Exercise 11

Identify each clause in the following sentences as independent or dependent.   Then determine whether each sentence is simple, compound, complex, or compound-complex.

   1. Some fishermen locate schools of fish by devices similar to those used for detecting enemy submarines.
   2. Plastic machine parts run silently, yet they need little or no oiling.
   3. Although the fans booed and threw lemons, Babe Ruth hit one of the longest homers that has ever been recorded.
   4. We arrived in Germany on June 27, and one of the first things that we did was head for the Mosel to taste wines and eat fresh trout.

5. To prevent piracy, manufacturers of computer programs have spent much time developing systems that have "copy protection."

6. Giddons, who wrote his first novel at age twenty, had made his reputation by age thirty; but he accomplished nothing after he turned forty.

7e Exercise 12

Combine each of the following sets of sentences to create the kind of sentence indicated. If you have trouble punctuating the combined sentences, see Chapter 21 and Chapter 22.

EXAMPLE: She grew tired of the incessant gossip. She slipped quietly off from the group. (simple) → She grew tired of the incessant gossip and slipped quietly off from the group.

1. The programmers worked for twenty-one hours without a break. They managed to complete the project on time. (complex)

2. Helium appears in natural gas deposits. Helium appears in the atmosphere. (simple)

3. Hieroglyphics sometimes read from left to right. Usually, they read from right to left or top to bottom. (compound)

4. Pterodactyls could fly. They were not birds. They were reptiles. (compound–complex)

5. Speed reading is practical for easy material. Slower reading is more effective for complex, challenging works. (compound)

6. Ms. Bloom reported the missing funds. Ms. Bloom had stolen the money herself. (complex)

7. My great-grandfather was one of ten children. My great-grandmother was one of seven. (compound)

8. John Culhane was an aggressive skater. In one game he met his match. A burly defenseman bumped him to the ice five times. (compound–complex)

7e Exercise 13

The prose in the following passages is choppy, and the relationship between ideas is not always clear. Vary the sentence types to include simple, compound, complex, and compound-complex sentences.

1. Readers often have trouble understanding supernatural stories. The action may truly take place. The action may take place only in the narrator's mind. For example, the narrator of Poe's "The Fall of the House of Usher" verges on insanity. Readers do not know the truth about the strange events. The events take place in a gloomy mansion. The events take place in a decayed mansion. In Henry James's "The Jolly Corner," Brydon sees a ghost. Brydon pursues the ghost. Brydon thinks the ghost is physically real. But the reader wonders. Is the ghost real? Is the ghost a symbol of Brydon's inner being?

2. I have always loved Thanksgiving. I love turkey and dressing. I love family dinners. At family dinners, relatives get together. They eat, drink, and laugh. After dinner, they relax. They watch football games. They swap stories. I also love Thanksgiving for another reason. It is not commercialized. For instance, salesclerks don't dress up like Pilgrims. People don't feel obligated to buy presents. Parents aren't frantically looking for the last Pocahontas doll in town. Thanksgiving is the ideal holiday. It brings families together. It doesn't cost much money.

Part I: Review Exercises

Part I, Review Exercise A

Write sentences containing the following words and structures.

1. personal pronoun in the subjective case
2. personal pronoun in the objective case
3. indefinite pronoun
4. past participle
5. present participle
6. noun phrase
7. verbal phrase
8. past tense verb

Part I, Review Exercise B

Write a paragraph containing the following words and structures.

1. coordinate conjunction
2. subordinate conjunction
3. prepositional phrase
4. conjunctive adverb

Part I, Review Exercise C

Write sentences containing the following structures.

1. independent clause with transitive verb
2. independent clause with linking verb
3. independent clause with intransitive verb
4. dependent adjective clause
5. dependent noun clause
6. dependent adverb clause
7. elliptical clause

Part I, Review Exercise D

Write a paragraph containing the following structures.

1. compound sentence
2. complex sentence
3. compound-complex sentence

Part I, Review Exercise E

Match the underlined words in the passage with their grammatical descriptions listed here. The best way to approach the exercise is to divide the descriptions into groups. First look for all the nouns, then all the pronouns, then the adjectives, and so on.

1. singular common noun
2. plural common noun
3. possessive noun
4. personal pronoun in the subjective case
5. personal pronoun in the objective case
6. personal pronoun in the possessive case
7. relative pronoun
8. indefinite pronoun
9. positive adjective
10. comparative adjective
11. conjunctive adverb
12. adverb qualifier
13. -ly adverb
14. auxiliary verb
15. modal auxiliary verb
16. verb in the subjunctive mood
17. verb in the simple past tense
18. infinitive
19. participle used as an adjective
20. preposition
21. coordinating conjunction
22. correlative conjunctions
23. subordinating conjunction
24. determiner
25. expletive

There is an increasing disregard in this country for good manners. This problem is obvious in very glaring ways. For example, drivers display rude and obscene bumper stickers without regard for the sensibilities of other people. Talk-show hosts verbally attack their guests. Parents allow their children not only to misbehave in public but also to ignore rights and property of others. People use parking lots as garbage dumps—tossing away food wrappers, beer cans, and even disposable diapers.

Rudeness is also obvious in the demise of small courtesies. For example, in the past when I stopped to let a motorist out into a moving line of traffic, I always received a wave of thanks. Now, when I stop, motorists simply pull out in front of me with no acknowledgment of my gesture. When I hold a door open for people behind me, they seldom say "thank you" or even give me a nod. Recently, in a large discount store, I was in the checkout line behind a customer who had among his purchases a picture frame with cracked glass. When I called his attention to the damaged frame, he asked the clerk whether he could exchange it. Then after walking all the way across the store and getting another frame, he checked out—never thanking me or even looking at me. Furthermore, the clerk who checked him out acted as if this behavior were normal.

It did not occur to me that the problem might be the result of ignorance until one day in a college classroom. While returning papers, my instructor accidentally bumped a student's desk and said, "Excuse me." The student simply sat and said nothing. My instructor said, "Now, we're going to do this again. I bump into your desk and say, "'Excuse me.' You say, 'Certainly.'" Then she bumped into the desk again, apologized again, and the flabbergasted student said, "Certainly." The instructor said, "Very good. That's how it works."

That experience suggested to me that perhaps we need a television program to encourage better manners. Actors could demonstrate polite behavior, and then members of the audience could ask questions and make comments—but only if they said "please" and "thank you."

Part I, Review Exercise F

Match the underlined phrases and clauses in the passage below with their grammatical descriptions listed here. As with Exercise E, you can divide the descriptions into groups. First look for all the phrases, then the independent clauses, then the dependent clauses, and then the sentences.

1. infinitive phrase
2. gerund phrase
3. participial phrase
4. prepositional phrase
5. independent clause with an intransitive verb
6. independent clause with a transitive verb
7. independent clause with a linking verb
8. dependent adverb clause
9. dependent adjective clause
10. dependent noun clause
11. elliptical clause
12. compound sentence
13. complex sentence
14. compound-complex sentence

Advertising constantly bombards us with the message that pain is unnatural, and, as a result, we immediately tackle any ache with some kind of painkiller. Unfortunately, painkillers can be very dangerous. By deadening pain, they can conceal illness; thus, they may allow a serious problem to go undetected.

Actually, most pain is very normal; it results from everyday living— for example, from tension, lack of sleep and exercise, tight clothes, fatigue, and poor diet. Thus, we can relieve most of our pain with simple common sense. For instance, if the headache sufferer lies down and relaxes, the headache will usually go away, without pills that irritate the stomach's lining. A stuffy nose can often be relieved by a hot shower instead of an antihistamine, and the sufferer will be not only less groggy but also cleaner. Feet aching from a long day of abuse will feel better after a soak in warm water. The stomach is a very sensitive organ, which vibrates to surrounding noises, such as loud, pulsating music. A stomach problem, therefore, frequently responds favorably to a good dose of silence. Backaches are often the result of poor posture or strain. Thus, someone with recurring back pain may need to stand and sit up straighter—or at the very least stop lying face down to work algebra problems and watch television at the same time.

When these common-sense remedies work, we save ourselves money as well as wear and tear on the body. When they do not work, the pain continues. Then we know that it is time to see a doctor. Therefore, we really should not fear pain so intensely. In fact, when acting as an alarm system, pain is a very good friend.

PART II

Structural and Grammatical Problems

Chapter 8

SENTENCE FRAGMENTS

8a Exercise 1

Rewrite to eliminate the fragment in each group of words.

1. Mel Tillis, the country music star, has no trouble singing. Although he stutters when he speaks.
2. While arthritis rarely threatens life. It can be a frustrating, painful experience.
3. As we were strolling casually along a tree-lined boulevard. We were approached by a man begging for money.
4. The company was plagued with both personnel and equipment problems. Which finally resulted in bankruptcy.
5. Noise places strain on the mind. Because it interferes with speech and hearing.

8b Exercise 2

Revise the structures to eliminate fragments.

1. He lost a million dollars in just a few months. His cocaine habit ruining his financial judgment.
2. The car is a network of computer controls. Controls for improving performance and maintenance.
3. They bought color-coordinated exercise suits. With the intention of getting into shape.
4. Our agency has promoted the development of synthetic fuels. Fuels to eliminate a dependence on oil.
5. The slogan is often worn on a button. Or displayed on a bumper sticker.

6. The professor was trying to explain computer speeds. Speeds such as milliseconds, microseconds, and nanoseconds.
7. Pedestrians had to dash through the spray of the lawn sprinkler. Or walk around it, out into the road.
8. I swung at the third pitch. Grazing the ball as it hurtled past.
9. Athletes should drink water frequently. Before, during, and after sports activities.
10. The record for completed passes was held by Rupert Gonzales. The first college quarterback to be drafted this year.

8a–8b Exercise 3

Revise the following passage to eliminate fragments.

The bicycle has been used in wars since 1870, but rarely by the United States. The French first trying bicycles for scouting expeditions in the Franco-Prussian War. In 1875 when Italians tried maneuvers on bicycles. Because of the pneumatic tire, reduced weight, and the ability to be folded up. By World War I, European troops used bikes extensively on the front lines. When World War II broke out, soldiers on bicycles frequently seen in Europe and Asia. Yet American troops traveled by ships, planes, trucks, and trains. In Europe, soldiers used bicycles to destroy railroads and bridges behind German lines. And to move supplies when the motors of trucks and jeeps broke down. Bicycles, which helped the Japanese move through thick jungles to take over Malaya and Singapore. During the Vietnam War, the Viet Cong used bicycles to carry supplies. Because bicycles made little noise and seldom broke down. Perhaps American troops with their dependence on modern technology overlooked an effective vehicle—the bicycle.

Chapter 9

COMMA SPLICES AND
FUSED SENTENCES

9a–9e Exercise 1

Revise each comma splice or fused sentence by using the option indicated in brackets.

1. A weekend guest should send a house gift to the hosts it should be neither expensive nor comic. [comma and coordinate conjunction]
2. Columbus mistook a group of manatees for mermaids, in fact, a blubbery manatee looks like Grover Cleveland with a moustache. [semicolon]
3. What the people want is clear, they want maximum government services and minimum taxes. [colon]
4. The pizza parlor refused to take our order, we had requested a pizza with one-third pepperoni, one-fourth ground beef, and five-twelfths ham. [dependent clause]
5. Struggling with the English language, he was frustrated by the pronunciation of *though, bough,* and *through,* no logic seemed to help. [two sentences]

9a–9e Exercise 2

Revise each comma splice and fused sentence by one of the options described in 9a through 9e. Choose an option that produces an effective sentence.

1. Sweat is extremely important, it is the primary way the body cools itself.

2. In Paris, the first week of fashion shows is "closed," admittance is limited to professional buyers, the invited press, and privileged clients.

3. Bibliographies are arranged topically, chronologically, or alphabetically, however, the alphabetical arrangement is the most common.

4. My friend has little time to study the stock market consequently, he has invested in a mutual fund.

5. Compulsive gambling is a psychiatric disorder, few treatment centers exist.

6. Sometimes the operations manuals are too technical for students, then the lab assistants must interpret the instructions.

7. Some areas of Texas got two inches of rain, most of the state got only a trace.

8. Fiercely competing for audiences, the soap operas are shooting on location in exotic settings, in addition, the shows are featuring unrealistic plots involving international crime, natural disasters, and travel in outer space.

9a–9e Exercise 3

Revise the following passages to eliminate comma splices and fused sentences.

1. In Paris, travel by taxi is easy. Taxis are plentiful, there are numerous stands. You can go to the "Tête de Station," obviously, you should take the first taxi in line. Some private cars serve as taxis, however, before taking them, you should settle the price. The easiest way to get a taxi is through your hotel concierge or porter whoever summons the taxi should get a one franc tip.

2. Studying for most objective tests is very different from studying for essay tests. Objective tests usually require only a knowledge of facts, however, essay tests also require the ability to interpret.

   To study for objective tests, I put each fact to be learned on a 3 x 5 card then I arrange the cards in logical order. When I learn a fact, I put that card into a separate stack. Gradually, the "learned stack" becomes larger and larger, finally, it contains all the cards, and I am ready for my test.

   My method for essay tests is very different. I go through my textbook taking notes, then I combine them with my class notes.

From this composite set of notes, I make an outline. Next, I try to predict possible test questions and group appropriate headings from my outline under the questions, therefore, I am able to assemble information into meaningful units. Also, I can practice analyzing the information I must use on the test.

In short, studying for an objective test is like getting ready for a trivia match, however, studying for an essay test is like preparing for a debate.

Chapter 10

SUBJECT–VERB AGREEMENT

10a–10c Exercise 1

Choose the correct verb for each sentence, making sure that it agrees with its subject. The problems involve compound subjects and words intervening between subjects and verbs.

1. Either the bonds or the real estate (is/are) sufficient collateral for the loan.
2. An assortment of diamonds, emeralds, and sapphires (gleams/gleam) from the pendant.
3. Her coach and mentor (was/were) the only person she consulted.
4. On a tool bit, the clearance and relief angles, which are ground on the bit, (determines/determine) the quality of the work.
5. France, along with Germany and Italy, (produces/produce) most European wines.
6. The second major section of the balance sheet, the liabilities, (lists/list) the debts that the company must pay.
7. Organization and planning (is/are) the key requirements for a successful recording session.
8. Clouds of red clay dust (has/have) settled on the fields.
9. The students or the professor (has/have) confused the examination date.
10. My roommate, together with three friends, (is/are) giving me a birthday dinner.

10d–10e Exercise 2

Choose the correct verb for each sentence, making sure it agrees with its subject—an indefinite or a relative pronoun.

1. Neither of the labor leaders (was/were) willing to negotiate further.
2. Winston Brown is one of those journalists who (satirizes/satirize) politics.
3. None of the instruction manuals fully (explains/explain) the procedure.
4. Each of the techniques reviewed in this report (requires/require) further research.
5. Pair ice-skating is the only one of the Olympic events that (suggests/suggest) romantic love.

10f–10g Exercise 3

Choose the correct verb for each sentence, making sure it agrees with its subject. The problems involve linking verbs and subjects that follow verbs.

1. The main expense (was/were) supplies, such as balsam, droppers, and Bunsen burners.
2. In the 1940s, all along the highway (was/were) sequences of Burma-Shave signs.
3. There (has/have) been six accidents at this intersection in three months.
4. My parents' main concern (is/are) my grades.
5. Hanging in her closet (was/were) three fur-lined coats.

10h Exercise 4

Choose the correct verb for each sentence, making sure the verb agrees with its subject—a collective noun or an amount.

1. The jury (disagrees/disagree) with public opinion.
2. The number of accidents (has/have) decreased since the new drunk-driving laws have been in effect.

3. Nine weeks (is/are) a sufficient time to complete the exit ramps.
4. The crew (is/are) wearing their new uniforms.
5. Six tons of crushed shells (was/were) used in the project to prevent erosion.

10i–10l   Exercise 5

Choose the correct verb for each sentence, making sure it agrees with its subject—a title, a foreign noun, a noun ending in *-ils,* or a word used as a word.

1. *Six Years with Cecil* (is/are) a new novel by Sarah Hughes.
2. "Politics (make/makes) strange bedfellows."
3. Sometimes, the media (seem/seems) to revel in tragedy.
4. The acoustics in the new auditorium (is/are) not good.
5. *Cattle* (has/have) no singular form.
6. Ballistics, which (is/are) the study of projectiles, has become a highly intricate discipline.
7. The bases of the argument (seems/seem) to be rather petty.
8. Niagara Falls (is/are) a breathtaking sight.
9. When I was a child, "The Three Little Pigs" (was/were) my favorite story.
10. In most of the junk mail I receive, "free gifts" (appears/appear) at least ten times.

10a–10l   Exercise 6

Correct any errors in subject–verb agreement in the following passage.

The only one of life's rules that have no exceptions is this: the other lane or line always move faster than the one you are in. Let's take, for example, my drive into town every morning. There are studies in "lane theory" that suggests that the left lane is preferable because people usually keep right. When I leave my house in the mornings, I pull into the closer lane: the left. For a few minutes I cruise along at a rapid pace. Suddenly in front of my car is about fifty drivers moving at 20 miles per hour. At this point cars in the right lane begins zipping past me like jackrabbits. I move quickly into the right lane, which slow immediately to a near halt. And so on it goes until I arrive at my destination, exhausted and frustrated.

Or take my weekly visit to the grocery store. After I've collected my groceries, I start evaluating the ckeck-out lines. There is three things I consider: Does the check-out person move fast? How full is the baskets of the customers? How many people are in the line? Then I make a choice. Sometimes all the factors is in my favor: the person at the register is hustling, and three people with only a few purchases are ahead of me. But does my deliberations pay off? No. The first person in line has an item that is not priced, so someone working in the store walk down eight aisles, find the item price, and return to report. The second of the three customers want to write a check for $3.20 on a bank in another country, and the manager must be called to stare at the check and the customer for five minutes. The third customer has a large envelope full of coupons to sort through. As it turns out, six people with seventy-five dollars worth of groceries apiece gets through the line next to me while I have been standing in mine.

And let's take banks. At the drive-in window, I always get behind one of those people who is doing the daily deposits of businesses. Inside the bank, I get behind a crowd who is obtaining travelers' checks, wrapping coins into paper cylinders, or wiring money to Canada.

Since I cannot escape my fate, I am going to change my habits. I will leave home in the morning a half hour early and put books in my purse to read while standing in lines.

Chapter 11

NONSTANDARD VERB FORMS

11a Exercise 1

Correct any errors in the forms of verbs.

1. The man had dove off the bridge before he could be stopped.
2. The committee give the award to an Egyptian writer.
3. The earthquakes have shook the hotel on five different occasions.
4. We seen the movie that was nominated for an Academy Award.
5. Their boat is sank a mile from shore.
6. All the silver and jewelry had been took in the robbery.
7. The whole turkey was ate at dinner.
8. Have you chose your tennis partner?

11b Exercise 2

In the following passage, add *-s/-es* and *-d/-ed* endings on verbs and verb forms where necessary.

I have a friend who insist that she never sleeps over three hours a night and thinks she is suppose to sleep about eight hours. Since I use to have the same problem, I suggested a few steps she might take before she waste money on a sleep-therapy course that cost $300.

First, anyone rest better when completely relax. Therefore, an insomniac should stop worrying about sleep because worry increase tension. Second, if a sleepless person resist eating spicy foods (such as barbecue potato chips and pizza), sleep will be more peaceful. Also, going to bed at a fix time helps develop a rhythm and makes it easier to fall asleep. In case everything else fail, there are always sheep to count.

11c Exercise 3

Look up the following pairs of words in the Glossary of Usage at the end of this textbook. For each word, write a sentence that illustrates its meaning.

1. advise/advice
2. censor/censure
3. device/devise
4. ensure/insure
5. lie/lay
6. sit/set

11c Exercise 4

Choose the correct word for each sentence.

1. The Vietnam War had a profound (affect/effect) on the generation of the 1960s.
2. The weak connection caused the transmitter to (lose/loose) power.
3. The "Delta" refers to the region that (lays/lies) between the Mississippi and the Yazoo rivers.
4. (Lie/Lay) this quilt across the foot of the bed.
5. By her facial expression, she (implied/inferred) more than she actually said.

11a–11c Exercise 5

In the following passage, insert the correct past and past participle forms of the verbs called for. Pay particular attention to irregular verbs and verbs easily confused with other words. Also, be sure to retain the -*d*/-*ed* ending on verbs like *used (to)*.

Last Saturday, a crowd of several hundred gathered to watch the demolition of the old Edgewater Beach Hotel, a structure that had (stand) for more than a hundred years. In the nineteenth century, the Edgewater had (be) a gathering place for the idle rich. In the twentieth, it had (see) elderly couples reliving their youth, teenagers attending basketball tournaments, and even the wrath of Hurricane Camille. Last Saturday, the demolition crew was (suppose) to destroy it so that a new Sears store could be (build) in its place.

On Friday the crew had (set) the charges. And on Saturday the crowd gathered to cheer for the Edgewater, expecting in some vague way that she might defy this onslaught as she (use) to defy tourists, teenagers, and hurricanes for decades.

The crew (put) on their hard hats, (wave) the crowd back to a safe distance, and (detonate) the charges. Nothing (happen). The Edgewater (stand) fast. The crowd (cheer) madly.

For three hours, the crew (reset) the charges. A strange hush (lie) over the crowd. No one (leave). Finally, the crew (signal) again. The levers (go) down. The Edgewater (shudder), then (shake), but (stand). A great roar (burst) from the crowd. Then people (begin) to sing "We Shall Overcome." But they had (forget) the deadly certainty of technology.

The crew (dive) in again. And after hours of labor, they (blow) down the Edgewater. She (sink) into a pile of rubble.

Chapter 12

PRONOUN REFERENCE

12a–12c Exercise 1

Revise the following sentences to correct any errors in implied, broad, or indefinite pronoun reference.

1. The fabric can be cleaned, but it must be done by a professional.
2. Keep the steps short, and do not combine them. This simplifies the job of converting the steps into a chart.
3. In many states, they do not require a test for the renewal of a driver's license.
4. It says in the article that the number of "reentry" students is increasing rapidly.
5. You can give pills to a dog by hiding them in hot dogs, which is called the "hollow-weenie" method.
6. Although society attempts to educate and reform the criminal, this is largely unsuccessful.
7. The Keeshond has been a guard dog for centuries, unlike other breeds that have recently been trained for it.
8. The information was not available, which forced the researcher to make an educated guess.
9. Vary the size of the letters. That will break the monotony.
10. Consumers like microwave ovens; this is evident from the sales figures.

12d–12e Exercise 2

In the following sentences, correct any errors in ambiguous pronoun reference and in the mixed uses of *it*.

1. My job at Jiffy Car Wash was to take the hubcaps off the wheels and wash them.
2. When Max received the award for outstanding athlete, it was obvious that he expected to win it.
3. I threw my radio against the window and shattered it.
4. The chef told the headwaiter that his job was not to flatter customers.
5. He wrote the song "Take My Love or Take a Bus." It said in the interview that it was for a country-and-western band that he wrote it.
6. Insert the ear attachments of the stethoscope in your ears so that they tilt slightly forward.
7. Some parents resort to extreme punishments because they work.
8. Because of the poor sales of the soft drink, the company said that it was important to withdraw it from the market.

12a–12g Exercise 3

Revise the following passage to ensure that all pronoun references are clear.

The Typewriter Keyboard

The most conventional one is called "Qwerty," after the first six keys of the third row from the bottom. It was designed in 1873 to slow typists down, because the keys stuck if they went too fast.

Sticking keys are no longer a problem, and a better system is needed. Patented in 1936, the Dvorak-Dealy keyboard reduces fatigue and increases speed, which makes it more efficient. The most commonly used keys are on the second row from the bottom—vowels and punctuation on the left, consonants on the right. This reduces the distance that the fingers must cover. In fact, with the Dvorak-Dealy system, typists' fingers travel about one mile a day; with the Qwerty system, they move their fingers about eighteen miles a day.

With the increase in computer use, more and more people are learning to type. Perhaps if manufacturers would offer the Dvorak-Dealy system as an alternative keyboard, it would be possible that someday all typists would change to it.

Chapter 13

PRONOUN–ANTECEDENT AGREEMENT

13a–13e Exercise 1

Rewrite the following sentences to make pronouns and antecedents agree and to avoid sexist language.

1. Each salesperson and each manager must submit their job description annually.
2. Neither the faculty members nor Dean Harper gave their approval to the new curriculum.
3. Everyone on board the ship had saved money for more than five years to pay for their passage.
4. A civil engineer should make sure that he has a thorough knowledge of architectural history.
5. When the jury delivered their verdict, reporters raced from the courtroom.
6. Did the popcorn or the pretzels have its ingredients listed on the package?
7. Both the angler fish and the stargazer have "lures" to attract its prey.
8. Every citizen should keep informed about how their tax money is spent.
9. A nurse under stress may do their job inefficiently and unsafely.
10. The Cadillac or the Buick is supposed to have their transmission fixed today.

13a–13e Exercise 2

Revise the following passage to ensure that pronouns and antecedents agree.

Because Shakespeare wrote for his audience, we can learn much about his plays by looking at the people who attended the Globe Theater. The average theatergoer did not question the social or political system, in which everyone knew their place. They had inherited a belief in an ordered universe. And yet that order was threatening to collapse. Both the aristocrat and the commoner in Shakespeare's day began to think that his ordered world might be shattered.

This conflict was partially responsible for the excellence of Shakespeare's work. Theodore Spencer suggests that great tragedy is written in periods when a person's patterns of behavior and their beliefs are threatened. Probably neither the theatergoers nor Shakespeare realized how soon their social order would collapse. But they were aware of the conflict. And in the conflict were some of the components of Shakespeare's remarkable plays.

13a–13e Exercise 3

Revise the following passage to eliminate sexist language. Make sure that in your revision each pronoun agrees with its antecedent.

The Cooperative Education Program allows the student to alternate his academic study with periods of work related to his major. Trained advisors assist the student in securing employment that will provide him with practical work experience as well as financial aid to support his education. Any student with an overall GPA of 2.50 is eligible to enter the program after he has completed forty-five hours. An applicant should submit the names of four character references, including at least one member of the business community, who must write his assessment of the student's employment potential.

Chapter 14

CASE OF NOUNS AND PRONOUNS

14a Exercise 1

For each sentence, choose the pronoun in the appropriate form.

1. According to the *Old Farmer's Almanac,* which my father and (I, me) have always relied on, March 5 will be flannel-pajama weather.
2. In the Chinese restaurant, Luke and (I, myself) got the same fortune cookie message: "Big Luck to Big Tippers."
3. My grandmother decided to divide her property between (he, him) and (I, me).
4. The credit for the team's performance must go to two people, the coach and (he, him).
5. The attendant told Mr. Ford and (she, her) that the flight had been delayed.

14b Exercise 2

In each sentence, choose the form of the pronoun appropriate in formal writing.

1. It wasn't (I, me) who recommended the course.
2. The best violinist in the orchestra is (she, her).
3. The employee who most often used the microfiche machine was (he, him).
4. It was (they, them) who wrote the script.
5. They discovered that it was (I, me) who had called.

14c Exercise 3

Insert *who, whoever, whom,* or *whomever* in each of the following sentences. (Remember to base your decision on the use of the pronoun in its own clause.)

1. The conference will be attended by those _____ teach psychology in senior colleges.
2. The position should be filled by someone _____ our clients will trust.
3. Show this pass to _____ is at the gate.
4. He is the actor _____ they say the director slapped.
5. The delegation met with the Prime Minister, _____ they assumed was in a position to make decisions.
6. Do you know someone _____ we can ask?
7. You can get through a class reunion by saying "You look fantastic!" to _____ you don't remember.
8. My grandmother knew a man _____ groomed Teddy Roosevelt's horse.
9. _____ stole my car now owns a gas guzzler that breaks down every fifteen miles.
10. _____ did he say wrote that novel?

14d Exercise 4

Supply the correct pronouns in the following sentences. If either the subjective or objective case is possible, explain why.

1. Anyone in the department can edit the report as well as (I/me).
2. A monarchy is not an appropriate government for people such as (they/them).
3. She writes about Jefferson as well as (he/him).
4. Mr. Thames, rather than (she/her), should present the achievement award.
5. We understood their ideas better than (they/them).

14e Exercise 5

Make the following sentences formal. Change nouns and pronouns to the possessive case where necessary.

1. The lecturer discussed Napoleon crowning himself emperor.
2. The reader tires of him constantly whining about life's injustices.
3. We are concerned over the project getting funded.
4. The State Department objected to them traveling to Libya.
5. Your host will appreciate you arriving on time.

14a–14e Exercise 6

Revise the following passages to correct any errors in noun or pronoun forms.

1. Whenever my neighbors get a new dog, they get a terrier who they always name Fido. This habit is almost as old-fashioned as my father naming his dog Rover. One man who I know called his dogs clever names like Go Away and Let Go. Between you and I, these silly names would embarrass any decent, self-respecting dog. Then, there are the American Kennel Club members, to who we are indebted for such names as Jo-Ni's Red Baron of Crofton, Sir Lancelot of Barvan, and St. Aubrey Dragonora of Elsdon.

   My brother and me have a solution to all this nonsense. We favor names like Sam and Jake for our dogs. You can't find more sensible names than them, and sensible animals deserve sensible names.

2. We began the study in fall 1985 at the University Sleep Center. The subjects were divided into two groups—one monitored by Dr. Patricia Goldin and myself, the other by a team of Austrian researchers. The participants who Dr. Goldin and me worked with were all under thirty years of age. None of the subjects objected to us monitoring them breathing during deep and twilight sleep. The subjects who we monitored recorded their breathing habits during waking hours. Dr. Goldin divided the collected data between the Austrian team and I for analysis.

Chapter 15

Nonstandard Adjective and Adverb Forms

15a Exercise 1

Choose the correct adjective or adverb for each sentence. When in doubt about the correct choice, look up the options in the Glossary.

1. The linguini tastes (good, well).
2. I feel (bad, badly) about the mistake.
3. The health farm is a (real, really) expensive resort.
4. It (most, almost) always rains during the first two days of our annual rodeo.
5. The child reads exceptionally (good, well).
6. The steak was (bad/badly) burned.
7. If we are going to perform well, we must practice (regular, regularly).
8. She spoke so (quiet/quietly) that I could not hear her.
9. The employees felt (bitter/bitterly) about the layoff.
10. Our test was (awful/awfully) hard.

15b Exercise 2

In the following sentences, correct any errors in the comparative and superlative forms of adjectives and adverbs.

1. German shepherds are the more dependable of all the popular guide dogs for the blind.
2. The Smithsonian is the most complete of the two museums.
3. The grass on the front lawn is deader than that on the back.
4. The new missile is more faster than its predecessor.
5. The mainest thing to remember is that the clutch doesn't work.

15a–15c Exercise 3

Revise the following passage to correct any adjective or adverb errors.

In used to be real awkward for me to leave a party. I would have the most hardest math test the next day and need to study, but I couldn't find a polite way to leave. Every time I was the first person to go, people would say they felt badly that I did not have a good time or that I should wait to hear their new guitar. These kind of remarks drove me crazy.

For a while, I tried two excuses. The best one was that I had to leave to let my dogs out of the house. The worst was that a spell of nausea had overtaken me very sudden. But no one took them excuses serious.

The silly thing is that most of the time, people don't actually care when I leave. They are merely being nice. So now I simply leave rapid before anyone notices that I am gone.

Chapter 16

DANGLING AND MISPLACED MODIFIERS

16a (1) Exercise 1

Rewrite the following to correct the dangling verbal phrases.

1. Caught in a rip current, it is important for a swimmer not to panic.
2. Enough French can be learned to ask common questions by using a conversation guide.
3. Beating Milwaukee, a well-deserved trophy was won by the Celtics.
4. By awarding scholarship money, potential nurses will be encouraged.
5. Adequate funds must be available in campaigning effectively for a candidate for governor.
6. Blowing from the north, the bay was kicking up whitecaps from the wind.
7. To learn more about the Loch Ness monster research, annual reports of the Loch Ness Phenomena Investigation Bureau can be studied.
8. To be an effective chip, most experts say that it must operate in either parallel or serial mode.
9. By blending Hollywood glamour and soul music, the direction of American music has been changed by Motown.
10. Based on this growing interest, the department has become more specialized.
11. After ascending the English throne, French became the language of government.
12. To avoid confusion, it is necessary to organize the balance sheet properly.

16a (2) Exercise 2

Revise the following sentences to eliminate dangling elliptical clauses.

1. Once redecorated, there was a pleasant atmosphere in the office.
2. Although annoyed by his attitude, his argument was convincing.
3. When repeating the story, a few details were added to make it more gruesome.
4. While making the meringue, the pie should be set aside to cool.
5. If enrolling in the class, it is recommended that you know Fortran.

16b Exercise 3

Rearrange or rewrite the following sentences to eliminate the misplaced and squinting modifiers.

1. We went to a movie about a criminal that was considered controversial.
2. The Sahara Desert is the largest desert in the world, which stretches across North Africa from the Atlantic Ocean to the Dead Sea.
3. Mrs. Jones decided to hang two swords that had belonged to her father on the wall.
4. The soap opera that we watch often has characters suffering from amnesia.
5. McLemore wrote that the computer would probably arrive on Tuesday in a letter.
6. The fisherman decided on the dock to clean the fish.
7. A therapy session will be held for students who have crises from 5:00 to 7:30 p.m.
8. The Nobel Prize winner for chemistry almost received enough money to retire.
9. The sailboat moving through the water slowly came into view.
10. As an adult dog, I expect my golden retriever to be well mannered and obedient.
11. Johnson tried always to have a lot of money in his account.
12. The police officer who was summoned immediately arrested the suspect.
13. The author said that he opposed taxation on property in the first chapter.
14. The computer only has one disk drive.
15. My instructor gave the class notes on how to design a title page that I now had to consult.

16a–16b .Exercise 4

Revise the following passages to eliminate dangling and misplaced modifiers.

1. For a ranch hand, a cowboy hat is practical. Using a cowboy hat for a variety of everyday needs, life can be simplified. When wearing the hat, the sun cannot burn the skin. Filled with water, a drinking cup is made. Also, when on horseback, a hat can be used as a whip.

2. Bad dreams about school are common. Entering the classroom to take a final, suddenly horror strikes. The dreamer is wearing no clothes. In another typical dream, the dreamer only gets to class to find the door locked. People have said often in their dreams that they oversleep and miss all their exams. Or while racing through the halls, there is the sudden realization that a forgotten research paper is due.

Chapter 17

SHIFTS

17a Exercise 1

The following passage has consistent present time. Rewrite it in past time by changing the italicized verb forms. Begin by changing the first verb to *were taught* and then make the rest consistent.

The children *are taught* in a practical and interesting fashion. For example, they *study biology* by collecting water samples and aquatic plants from a small pond. They *study* fractions by playing computer games with graphic representations as well as numbers. They even *learn* acceptable social behavior by role-playing conventional etiquette and manners. In other words, the students actively *participate* in their own education, and thus they *gain* real knowledge at a young age.

17a Exercise 2

Rewrite the passage in Exercise 1 above so that the italicized verbs suggest ability or recommendation rather than fact. Begin by changing the first verb to *could be taught*, and then make the rest consistent.

17a Exercise 3

In the following passage, the verb sequence is inconsistent. Change the inconsistent verbs and modal auxiliaries to place the passage (a) in present time and then (b) in past time.

If you want the cornbread light and fluffy, you could let all the ingredients come to room temperature before you mix the batter. That way, the raw batter would rise slightly in the bowl and would contain more air.

17a (4) Exercise 4

The following paragraphs discuss two characters in the novel *Lord of the Flies*. The writer begins in the historical present but then inappropriately shifts some of the verbs. Revise to make the verb sequence consistent.

Throughout the novel, Ralph stands for order and reason. His right-hand man is Piggy, the intellectual of the group. Ralph and Piggy took a practical approach to the predicament, trying to maintain a signal fire and to build shelters. They started the fire by using a lens of Piggy's glasses. The suggestion is that the glasses brought fire, or light, symbolic of knowledge.

Jack is also practical to a point. He organizes the hunters and kills wild pigs for food. But the hunts soon became a ritual. The hunters painted their faces with colored clay, and they danced and chanted after the killings. Jack's right-hand man is Jack, a sadist and murderer.

17b Exercise 5

Some of the following infinitive and participle forms are correct and some are not. Point out the correct forms. Then revise the incorrect forms to make verb sequence logical.

1. Driven by greed, the financiers created monopolies.
2. The game was supposed to have begun at 7:00.
3. She hopes to have finished the report by tomorrow.
4. After melting the plastic, we poured it into molds.
5. After melting the plastic, we pour it into molds.
6. We should have planned to have reached the restaurant before noon.
7. I would like to have heard his speech last week.
8. Making reservations in February, we had front-row seats in April.

17c–17d Exercise 6

Revise the following sentences to correct shifts in mood and voice.

1. The dictionary lists the most common part of speech first, and the most frequent meaning is given as the first definition.

2. If the diver were equipped with the new tank, he can stay underwater for eight hours.
3. The litigants will have spent thousands of dollars before an agreement will be reached.
4. In emergencies, pause, and then you should take a couple of deep breaths.
5. By providing a puppy with the proper atmosphere, you can promote good habits; and then trainability can be established.
6. If I can go to bed earlier, I would get more done during the day.

17e–17f Exercise 7

Revise the following sentences to correct any shifts in person and number.

1. Don't submit your manuscripts in ornamental binders; students should put their manuscripts in plain folders or boxes.
2. A traveler should consult several guides. Travelers who do no research are sure to miss many opportunities.
3. These four courses require a one-hour lab.
4. You will find the microcomputer especially valuable when you prepare proposals. The writer can easily pull together previously stored date.
5. At first, math teachers objected to the student use of pocket calculators. Now, however, a math teacher usually sees the value of one.

17g–17h Exercise 8

Revise the following sentences to correct mixed constructions (faulty predication) and shifts between direct and indirect discourse.

1. The Renaissance was when people began to emphasize classical art and culture.
2. Garbage as an energy source is a capacity to save money.
3. The lady protested indignantly, "What do you mean, you won't take dogs" and that her Fifi would never stay in a kennel.
4. The reason he quit his job was because he wanted to move to Florida.
5. Nancy Wells, a high school English teacher, said "a parade should have bands *or* horses" but that it should not have both.

6. A bank is where they loan you money if you can prove you don't need it.
7. The study concluded a need for early detection of alcoholism.
8. The reduction of the car's weight is an idea that will reduce fuel consumption.
9. Every year, gun control laws get more heated.
10. Poor attendance and bad reviews were the early cancellation of the play.
11. An implosion is when an object bursts inward.
12. The reason for the boycott was because the company charged too much rent.

17h Exercise 9

Write three sentences expressing a reason and three expressing a definition. Make sure you do not create an illogical shift by writing *reason is because, something is when, a place is where.*

17a–17h Exercise 10

Revise the passage to eliminate shifts. The shifts may occur in tense; with *can/could, will/would;* in mood, voice, number, or person; between direct and indirect discourse; and in mixed constructions (faulty predication).

There is a movement today to make the curricula of schools more demanding. The reason is because American schools are now being compared to the rigorous Japanese schools and were found lacking. Therefore, students cannot find crib, or gut, courses as easily as you once could. Supposedly, credit once could be gotten by students for Basketweaving 101 or Relaxation I. Now, such courses are rare. With a careful strategy, however, you could still find a few courses that will not strain your brain or tax your time.

First, a student can find out which courses would be recommended for the athletes. For example, if you had heard a geology course referred to as "Rocks for Jocks," you know it has possibilities. Also, another possibility might be a course for elementary education majors. At registration, look for a course in poster painting or construction paper art.

Also, you can search for files and guides kept by organizations. One fraternity's file is named "Micks," short for Mickey Mouse. According to one member, "The Micks file is the one most often used" and that it is constantly kept up to date.

Another strategy is where you look for special kinds of titles in the school catalog. With something called "Highlights of . . ." is a good bet. The use of "Basics of . . ." and "Fundamentals of . . ." also explains that the courses probably required little effort.

Since the search for crib courses has gotten harder, use these suggestions to ensure a painless education. If a student cannot locate enough easy courses to fill out a schedule, you might have to break down and study.

Chapter 18

SPLIT CONSTRUCTIONS

18a–18d Exercise 1

Revise the following sentences to eliminate awkward and unclear split constructions.

1. If you default on mortgage payments, the lender can, according to the general rule of mortgage law, foreclose on your property.
2. Warm Springs, Georgia, where Franklin D. Roosevelt went to try to recover the use of his legs in the warm baths, is now a rehabilitation center.
3. Whatever the English architects imported, they changed it to, with great inventiveness, fit the British climate and temperament.
4. The first mechanical adding machine was, surprisingly in 1642, invented by Blaise Pascal when he was just a teenager.
5. The focus of genetic research in agriculture has been to safely increase yield and to effectively make plants resistant to disease and damage.
6. To make computer chips, engineers first draw, by hand or by a computer, maps of the electrical circuit.
7. Cats and villagers in the 1950s in Japan developed after eating fish contaminated by mercury from a chemical plant a nervous disorder dubbed the "dancing cat" disease.
8. Elvis Presley was, according to Tom Wolfe, a "Valentino for poor whites."
9. Rudolf Flesch, the author of numerous books on reading and what Flesch calls "readability," has devised a formula that measures the reading level of prose.
10. Portions of the Conewago River were unable to satisfactorily support the reproduction of trout.

18a–18d Exercise 2

Revise the passage to eliminate awkward or unclear split constructions.
You may decide that some of the split constructions are acceptable.

In high school, I with insistence from my parents, took French. I had no
idea why they had at this time demanded that I learn a foreign language. No one around me spoke French. Anyway, I obediently enrolled,
but there was no incentive to industriously and enthusiastically study.
France was very far away, and I had in my wildest dreams no idea of
ever meeting a native.

I, you might guess, did not apply myself to learning. I did, however,
come to intensely love the sound of French; it can make the dullest
statements sound romantic and interesting. But I after weeks and
weeks of struggling could never master the *r* in the throat or the *n* or
m in the nose. Another problem was in some spoken phrases that the
French run words together. For example, *les hommes (the men)* when
it is spoken sounds like *layszumm*.

I could manage to without difficulty learn vocabulary like *boeuf* for
beef, porc for *pork,* and *juin* for *June.* But other words were with my
limited effort much harder to learn.

The worst problem was that the nouns are masculine or feminine.
The book (le livre) for some very strange reason is masculine; *the chair
(la chaise)* for an equally strange reason is feminine.

This summer I have a chance to visit Paris, and I, with real regrets
about not studying, will have to probably depend on sign language and
pity from the French to survive.

Chapter 19

INCOMPLETE CONSTRUCTIONS

19a–19b Exercise 1

Revise the following sentences by completing the compound constructions or by inserting *that* wherever necessary.

1. John Brookings added the loans by the bank had been excessive.
2. Many consumers are insisting and purchasing foods low in sodium, sugar, and fat.
3. The recent graduates said when they tried to get jobs, they had no success.
4. The budget cuts have proved the answer can come from financial control.
5. The writer and director we heard speak last year in New York will both be on the panel.
6. The course included familiarization and qualification on the M-16.
7. I read the indictment was not made public for three weeks.
8. The hotel has not and does not plan to charge guests for telephone calls.

19c Exercise 2

Make the changes necessary to eliminate any confusion that results from incomplete or illogical comparisons.

1. The computers at the library work so slowly.
2. They installed the most sophisticated stereo equipment.
3. The Washington Monument is nearer the Mall than the Lincoln Memorial.
4. Louisiana's shrimp season begins earlier than other Gulf states.

5. The Sears Tower in Chicago is taller than any building in America.
6. The jazz performance was such a brilliant one.
7. Cheese has far more fat.
8. The volcano is as dangerous, perhaps even more dangerous than, Mt. St. Helens.
9. The damage done by the water was more serious than the wind.
10. Few candidates have had their campaigns aided by as influential a politician as Mayor Nelson.

19a–19c Exercise 3

Revise the following passage to eliminate incomplete constructions.

Horse racing is more harmful to horses than any sport. I once considered it exciting, but now I have come to realize profits are more important to owners than the horses.

Races are scheduled so often. The owners do not take into consideration the general health of the horses may be endangered by fatigue. Even bad weather does not often cause cancellation of races.

Sometimes the racetrack surface is too hard. Horses' legs are more fragile than many other animals. Numerous injuries are caused and result from this physical abuse. Drugging horses is crueler. I have notice drugs like narcotics are still used at many racetracks. The horses run unaffected and unaware of pain.

Probably some owners treat their horses humanely. But others have never and will never consider the welfare of their horses to be as important, or more important than, profits.

Chapter 20

PARALLELISM

20a Exercise 1

Find and correct any examples of faulty parallelism in compound structures.

1. The book is divided into two sections—the first focusing on individuals and the second examines generalizations.
2. We wrote a letter intended to eliminate the confusion and which was apparently not received.
3. In temperament, not how he appeared, he resembled his mother.
4. The story is not only puzzling but also disturbs the ordinary reader.
5. As a fly ball is hit, a fielder must judge where the ball will come down and how fast to run to get there.
6. Future space explorations will require flights not of days but years.
7. I would rather suffer through a boring lecture than to miss out on important information.
8. We neither have the time nor the means to learn German before our trip.
9. The book covers information from the discovery of the site to when the artifacts were displayed in the Egyptian museum.
10. The campers were either in their cabins or eating in the mess hall.

20b Exercise 2

Correct the faulty parallelism in the following sentences.

1. I find your continuing chauvinistic attitude offensive, sophomoric, and simply displays the worst taste.

2. Computers are capable of programming, remembering, scanning, and they can sort information.
3. The author is a distinguished journalist, lecturer, and has written over fifteen books.
4. The most successful adults have learned to channel their energy, to empathize with others, and they fit into a suitable society.
5. A marketing research analyst has these duties:
   designing marketing research studies
   to interpret research results
   operating a research data retrieval system
   an analyst must monitor existing products

20a–20b Exercise 3

Fill in the blanks with words or phrases parallel to the other items in the sequences.

1. The songs have typical themes—broken hearts, lonely nights, and
   _____.
2. The program traces not only how we got involved in Vietnam but also _____.
3. A path winds through the woods, along a stream, and _____.
4. The store sells expensive but _____ books.
5. At the school I will learn either to use the word processor or
   _____.
6. He has a reputation for working hard but _____.
7. Many people do not know what a quark is or _____.
8. I will take a cut in pay rather than _____.
9. _____ and when you use credit cards, you must take special care not to overextend yourself financially.
10. How you take a photograph, not _____, will determine the quality of the result.

20a–20b Exercise 4

Revise the following passage to remove any faulty parallelism.

In football games, the job of the officials is not easy. They must be ready to react to such confusing plays as blocked kicks, fumbled snaps and catches, goal line plays, end zone plays, and whether a player is eligible.

They must be aware both of when a foul occurs and where the ball is at the time of the foul.

Officials not only must know all the rules but also be able to remember them instantly. They must cope with such complicated infractions as these:

> an illegal block by the fair catch caller
> when a player runs into or either roughs the kicker or holder
> when a player bats the ball forward in the field of play or backward out of the end zone
> a noncontact interference with the opportunity to catch a kick

No official can stop the game, get out the rule book, studying the details, and then calling the play.

The officials' job, though, is not just to call the plays on the field; officials must also deal with the players themselves. Players frequently play very aggressively, not in a cooperative mood. Officials must make sure that all players are under control and respecting the whistle which signals the end of a play. To ensure this control, officials must stay alert and being able to move quickly to the location of the infraction. Either the players must respond to this authority or be removed from the game.

The next time you disagree with an official or hear one booed by fans, take pity. It's hard work.

PART II: REVIEW EXERCISES

Revise the following compositions to remove all grammatical and structural errors. As you read, look specifically for

fragments (frag)
comma splices (cs)
fused sentences (fs)
subject-verb agreement errors
   (s-v agr)
nonstandard verb forms (vb)
pronoun reference errors (ref)
pronoun-antecedent agreement
   errors (pn agr)

pronoun case errors (case)
dangling or misplaced modifiers
   (dm/mm)
adjective-adverb confusion (ad)
split constructions (split)
shifts (shift)
faulty parallelism (//)
incomplete constructions (inc)

1. I began reading those "romance novels" last summer that are sold in drugstores and quick-stop groceries. Finally, after three months, I realized both that these books all tell the same story and have the same characters.

   Readers are first introduced to the heroine, who they are supposed to identify with. On page one, you see her in shabby clothing however, we know she was born an aristocrat because of her "aristocratic brow and regal bearing." As our story opens, we discover our heroines family is down on their luck. Although the young lady has been forced to work as a governess or music teacher to support an invalid mother or father. The family have rich (but haughty) relatives.

   Now the hero. He, or course, is one of the rich and haughty relatives who has shunned the heroines family. But the relationship is distant enough for him to marry the heroine eventually. The hero had black hair—and plenty of it. He also has black, "mocking" eyes and with muscles that show through his clothes.

   When the hero and heroine meet, this happens. She is rude to him because he is real arrogant, he is charmed by her "spirit." The plot unfolds. The heroine both despises and years for the hero. He, after becoming fatally smitten with her charms, "determines to have her." The reason is because she is "in his blood." In some of these kind of novels, the characters engage in steamy love scenes. In others, the author demurely notes when the heroine is near the hero, her "pulse quickens alarmingly." In the end, it's all the same. Hero marries heroine. Hero becomes doting wimp, heroine becomes rich.

After reading these literary clones, a plot of my own begun to take shape. Author of books tell same story over and over to wimpy readers; author gets rich.

2.   King Louis XIV of France commissioned La Salle to explore the Mississippi River and claim its great valley for France. La Salle organized an expedition in Canada and started down the Mississippi River in February 1682. La Salle's expedition, like many before and after it, made not only important discoveries but also encountered many misadventures and tragedies.

When La Salle reached the mouth of the river on April 9, 1682. He then planted the French flag and proclaimed that all lands of this great river valley belonged to Louis, King of France. In his honor, he named the new lands "Louisiana."

La Salle's next job was to fortify the mouth of the river to keep other nations out. After returning to France for supplies, soldiers, and men, the plan was to sail back to the mouth of the river by way of the Gulf of Mexico. Events begun to go awry immediately, on the trip the Spanish captured one of La Salle's four ships. Then, La Salle, suffering from a near fatal illness and misled by erroneous information about winds and currents in the Gulf, sailed too far west and misses the mouth of the river. Instead, they landed at Matagorda Bay on the Texas coast.

La Salle's troubles multiplied. Attempting to make camp ashore, he lost many of his provisions when his supply ship ran aground. Local Indians attached his camp, and also his hunting parties were harassed. Sending one of his two remaining ships back to France, La Salle set out cross-country with a small party of twenty men, he hoped to locate the mouth of the river. Unable to find it, he returned to his camp to learn that his only remaining ship had been run aground and destroyed.

Now stranded, he set out to feel his way toward Canada. On the way, his crew was weary, and La Salle became more despondent almost to the point of madness. This caused the crew to mutiny. After an argument, they murdered La Salle's nephew and two aides. Then to conceal these murders, he was killed. They buried him in the wilderness and walked back to Canada. Only five of the men made it to Canada. On the Texas coast, the settlers, who La Salle had left behind, were wiped out by the Indians and because they got diseases. France's first attempt to settle the Gulf Coast ended in failure.

PART III

Punctuation and Mechanics

Chapter 21

Commas

21a Exercise 1

In the following passage, insert commas where they are needed between independent clauses.

In the 1950s, there were a number of "quiz" shows on television. Contestants displayed a breadth of knowledge but most won very little money. Winning the game by displaying one's knowledge was the point. Now the quiz shows are gone and in their place have come "game" shows. Contestants don't need any knowledge to play yet they must have the ability to jump up and down and squeal. With this talent, they can win thousands of dollars or they can drive away in Cadillacs.

21a Exercise 2

Join each of the pairs of sentences with a comma and an appropriate coordinating conjunction (*and, but, or, nor, for, so,* and *yet*).

1. Classes were dismissed at noon. By 1:00, the campus was deserted.
2. I dropped out of school temporarily to get some experience in the business world. To put it another way, I ran out of money and had to work for a while.
3. We stayed in Florida for an entire week. The sun never came out once.
4. This course has no prerequisite. It can be taken anytime during the program.
5. In the past, children of divorced parents were said to come from "broken homes." Now these children are said to belong to "single parents."

21b (1) Exercise 3

In the following sentences, place commas where needed after introductory prepositional phrases.

1. In my family public displays of affection were discouraged.
2. During droughts the plant's roots reach deeper into the ground.
3. As an entering freshman I was intimidated by my professors, but after one semester in school I realized that most of them are helpful and not fearsome.
4. A representative of the group stated that without a good bit of government aid many area farmers would lose their farms this year.
5. By noon electricity had been restored.

21b (2) Exercise 4

In the following passage, insert commas where needed after introductory verbal phrases.

To solve the pollution problem each of us must accept our individual responsibility, and we might as well start with the kitchen sink, the place where most people store their household cleaners. By throwing away bottles and cans of hazardous, toxic, and corrosive cleaners we pollute the garbage and then a landfill. Leaking from the landfill the waste comes back home in the drinking water.

Through advertising manufacturers lead us to believe that we need powerful chemical cleaners in our homes. However, these cleaners are not really necessary. To clean ovens all we need is a mixture of salt and baking soda, both natural abrasives. Vinegar can replace ammonia-based cleaners for floors. Sprinkled with dry cornstarch and then vacuumed carpets become as fresh as those cleaned with commercial carpet cleaner. We can all help decrease pollution; by using the products on our kitchen shelves instead of those under our kitchen sinks we can be more responsible citizens.

21b (3) Exercise 5

In the following passage, insert commas where needed after introductory adverb clauses.

Even though the birthrate is increasing over half the population of the United States will soon be over fifty years of age. If we are to deal successfully with this new trend we must rethink our attitudes toward aging. In the past, most of us have believed that when we reach fifty we should also have reached all our goals. We cannot afford, however, to have 50 percent of our citizens without goals, without direction, without interest in the future. Life after fifty can be full of challenge and growth. But how?

Where there is learning there is growth. Once we stop trying to educate only our youth and start trying to educate the entire population we will make progress. Continued learning—at all ages—is the key to a full life and to a vital citizenry. As we have always heard youth can accomplish much with education. The same is true of those no longer young.

21b (4) Exercise 6

Put commas after the introductory noun clauses serving as objects and complements but not as subjects.

1. Whoever wishes to enjoy a cruise must also enjoy close quarters.
2. Whatever he said his assistant echoed.
3. Whomever the governor appoints the legislature must approve.
4. Whatever the animal is trained to be it will be.
5. Whatever the omens foretold was not questioned.

21c Exercise 7

In the following sentences, enclose the nonrestrictive clauses and phrases with commas.

1. James Savage who was my Shakespeare professor won the bass fishing rodeo for five straight years.
2. Students taking the word processing course must schedule laboratory time once a week.
3. Chicken soup sometimes called homemade penicillin actually has medicinal effects.
4. The musician Dylan seemed to be at odds with the poet Dylan.
5. The Civil War or the War of the Rebellion settled the question of whether a state could secede.
6. The first-string quarterback who sprained his knee in the first game was out for the season.
7. There is proverb that states, "Never eat at a place called Mom's and never play cards with a man named Doc."

8. Registration reminded me of the U.S. Army whose motto is "Hurry up and wait."
9. The student a computer buff since high school was arrested for selling bootlegged software.
10. Everyone I knew on the entire campus had gone home for the holidays.

21c Exercise 8

Combine each of the following pairs of sentences into one sentence containing a restrictive or nonrestrictive element. Indicate restrictive elements by the absence of commas and nonrestrictive elements by the presence of commas.

EXAMPLE: One of the jewels in the Triple Crown is the Kentucky Derby. The Derby is the best-known horse race in the country. → One of the jewels in the Triple Crown is the Kentucky Derby, the best-known horse race in the country.

1. Rhode Island is the smallest state in the Union. It is also an important industrial area.
2. The royal palm is a tropical tree. It resembles a pillar with a crown of leaves at its top.
3. The shallot is the best of the sauce onions. It is especially good in wine cookery.
4. I don't like digital watches. They look like machines instead of jewelry.
5. My father has an excellent sense of direction. He can find his way through any city with ease.
6. I try to take courses from certain professors. These professors don't assign research papers.
7. The game of hockey began in the 1800s. It became the national sport of Canada by the 1900s.

21c Exercise 9

Insert commas to enclose the nonrestrictive elements in the following passage.

The authenticity of Robin Hood who was a legendary English hero has been much disputed. He was popularized as Locksley a character in Sir

Walter Scott's fiction. But Robin appeared long before that. A few early historians have made claims that he lived in the 1100s. Also, he was mentioned in *Piers Plowman* a work written in the late 1300s. Furthermore, one of the earliest ballad collections that has been preserved is *Lytell Geste of Robyn Hoode* which was printed in 1495.

In most sources, Robin lives in Sherwood Forest which is located in Nottinghamshire. He leads a band of colorful outlaws who spend their time robbing the rich and giving to the poor.

Probably not much of the myth is true. Yet Robin's "grave" is supposedly located in Yorkshire where his bow and arrow are exhibited.

21d (1) Exercise 10

In the following sentences, insert commas between items in a series.

1. As a child, he liked to read stories about the American wilderness the exploration of the frontier and the Indian wars.
2. The primary staples of their diet were cornbread chicken rice and gravy.
3. I buy clothes that are washable wrinkle-free and reduced.
4. Either the schedule was wrong the train was late or I was in the wrong terminal.
5. The elegant auction featured diamond jewelry ancient jade statues and furniture.

21d (2) Exercise 11

In each series of modifiers, insert commas between coordinate adjectives but not between noncoordinate adjectives.

1. a spacious elegant Italian provincial house
2. the first four years of school
3. a smooth delicate cheese sauce
4. a cold gray rainy afternoon
5. many happy carefree lazy summer vacations

21d Exercise 12

In the following passage, insert commas between items in a series and coordinate adjectives.

When taking photographs with people as subjects, most amateur photographers do not pay enough attention to the horizon the position of the subjects or the framing. You can easily solve these problems.

First, make sure that the horizon is not tilted that it does not dominate the picture and that it does not split the picture in half. Next, position your subjects so that the picture seems evenly lit. Place subjects where the sun hits them from the side put them in the shade against an uncluttered background or put them in filtered muted lighting.

Finally, check the edges of the photograph fill the whole area with what you are shooting and eliminate as much background as possible. To make your subject or subjects more interesting, include something interesting in the foreground: a tree branch to suggest depth a stream that leads from the foreground to the background or a fence that the eye can follow.

21e Exercise 13

In the following sentences, use commas to indicate where verbs or parts of predicates have been omitted.

1. An African bull elephant weighs from 12,000 to 14,000 pounds; an Asian bull from 7,000 to 12,000.
2. The Brontë sisters shocked readers with their unusual stories: Emily with the eerie *Wuthering Heights;* Charlotte with the independent heroine of *Jane Eyre.*
3. The northern trade route ran from China across central Asia to Byzantium; the southern route from China to the Red Sea and overland to the Nile and northern Egypt.
4. During the day the temperature is over ninety; at night under sixty.
5. The ancestry of a purebred horse is traced through a single breed; the ancestry of a thoroughbred horse to three Arabian stallions—Darley Arabian, Godolphin Barb, and Byerly Turk.

21f (1) Exercise 14

In the following sentences, insert commas to set off parenthetical elements that function either as interrupters or as concluding remarks.

1. You should write a note after a job interview regardless of whether you want the job to thank the interviewer for his or her time.

2. Diary keeping at least for many people is a way of comparing dreams and realities.
3. The stereo speakers according to the instructions should be about 20 feet apart.
4. The reporter refused to reveal her sources because she wanted to protect their safety or so she said.
5. Wrinkles as a general rule are caused by the breakdown of collagen and elastin in the skin.

21f (2) Exercise 15

Use commas to set off the transitional expressions in the following passage.

While looking at some old photograph albums that had belonged to my mother, I was struck by how carefully she had documented her life. First there was her young adulthood with friends; then there were the early years of her marriage; and finally there were the stages of her children's lives. For example I saw her at high school dances and college football games. I saw her on her honeymoon at Niagara Falls. I saw my brother and me as infants, toddlers, grammar school brats, and teenagers.

Most of the pictures of course were amateurish. In addition many were blurred with age. Nevertheless that photograph album brought whole lives into focus. And more particularly it brought only the good times back. Consequently looking at the snapshots made me feel that life had been good to my mother and to her children.

As a result I have determined to take more photographs. I will naturally embarrass my children by running around with a camera, leaping from behind potted palms to immortalize them with a click. They will however thank me when they grow up—just as I now thank my mother.

21f (3) Exercise 16

In the following sentences, enclose the contrastive elements within commas whenever necessary.

1. Lately, it seems that football not baseball is the national pastime.
2. Living in Los Angeles unlike living in New York requires a car.
3. They provide guides for tours but only for walking tours.

4. The reflexive of *they is themselves* never *theirselves.*
5. This manual is a complete but not very readable guide to organic gardening.

21g Exercise 17

In the following speech, insert commas to set off interjections, words in direct address, and tag questions.

Ladies and gentlemen may I have your attention please. Thank you for coming tonight to hear our candidate for governor. Usually, all politicians are alike. We know how they operate don't we? They make promises they don't keep in return for our contributions—which they do keep. Well this candidate is a bit different. He's going to tell us what he might be able to do as governor. He isn't going to tell us thank goodness what he promises to do. And wonder of wonders he isn't going to ask us for any money. So friends please help me welcome this unique candidate won't you?

21h Exercise 18

In the following letter, use commas to punctuate dates, addresses, numbers, and titles.

9781 Ironwood Drive
Birmingham Alabama 35201
June 11 1996

Mr. Arnold Bennett President
Bennett and Hughes
8581 Indian Wood Road
Nashville Tennessee 37219

Dear Mr. Bennett:

One June 10 1996 we surveyed the proposed site for the bridle paths. The 10112-acre site can accommodate 23 miles of paths. The terrain seems ideal, varied but not dangerous. The area is scenic, with diverse plant life, small streams, and outcrops of rock.

We suggest that you have a feasibility study done to determine whether tourist access to the area is sufficient. We can recommend a reputable firm in Nashville, with an excellent history in feasibility and marketing studies. For information, write to

> Donald Shaw
> Adams and Cromwell
> 1919 University Place
> Nashville TN 37219

Sincerely yours,

L. Brett Carter

L. Brett Carter

21h (4) Exercise 19

Insert commas where appropriate to set off quotations from the words that identify their source.

1. "Remember that as a teenager" Fran Lebowitz said "you are in the last stage of your life when you will be happy to hear that the phone is for you."

2. According to H. L. Mencken "For every human problem, there is a neat, plain solution—and it is always wrong."

3. The report showed that employees were very dissatisfied with the classification system. Quite a few comments addressed that subject. For example, one employee said "The job levels are totally unfair, and moving from one level up to another is virtually impossible." Another complained "The salary increments for some levels do not allow for cost-of-living raises, much less for merit raises." Many employees felt that job levels did not reflect the responsibilities of the positions. "I am an assistant to two coordinators" said one person "and my responsibilities are administrative. Yet, the Office of Personnel classifies me as a clerk-typist, and I am paid accordingly."

21i Exercise 20

In the following sentences, insert commas for clarity.

1. No matter how late the message was welcome.
2. To the Burgundian beer drinkers are contemptible.
3. Any unlikely event that would destroy carefully laid plans if it did occur will occur.
4. With the extras added on the car can be purchased for about $23,000.
5. Those who can perform; those who cannot criticize.

21j Exercise 21

Remove any inappropriate commas from the following sentences.

1. The ball seemed to float toward the goalposts and, then remain stationary for several seconds.
2. The book that he assigned us, was too technical for novices.
3. My feet were sore, my back was aching, and, my head was swimming.
4. The announcement said, that the winner had been disqualified, and that the race would be rerun.
5. The realtor felt, that the property was valuable.
6. I think baton twirling is silly, although, I realize it takes a good bit of skill.
7. It was a slow, lazy, meandering, stream.
8. The dancer was not only graceful, but also remarkably athletic.
9. I thought I heard someone scream, that the stadium was on fire.
10. The people who lived next door, had eight cats and six dogs.

21a–21j Exercise 22

In the following composition, insert commas where they are needed, and delete commas where they are inappropriate. Some of the commas are properly placed.

Getting a summer job takes a good bit of planning, that must not be overlooked. First you must consider what kinds of jobs you are qualified for. For example if you cannot type you can rule out not only a secretarial position, but also a receptionist position which almost always involves some typing. Or if you are under twenty-one you cannot expect to land a job, that requires you to handle alcoholic drinks. In other words you must realistically assess your possibilities.

After this assessment you should consider whether there are any jobs you are simply unwilling to undertake. For example if you are not willing to work late at night on weekends and on the Fourth of July you should not apply at fast-food restaurants. No, a better job for you would be, with a local government, which would ensure you regular hours, and vacations on holidays.

When you have your abilities and preferences in mind the next step is to get yourself ready to accept responsibility. Come to terms with the fact that you cannot miss work because of late-night partying and you cannot expect other employees to do the work, that you have been hired to do. You must act, in other words like a mature responsible adult.

Once you are ready, psychologically ready to work you can begin your search. First you should check all want ads bulletin boards and radio programs that list jobs. Also you should register with the local state-employment agency for this service will not charge a fee for a job search. In addition if you can afford the cost you should apply with private employment agencies which usually charge a percentage of the first, month's salary.

The next step is, to contact people in your community who might act as references and recommend you to prospective employers. Everyone has heard that old expression, "It isn't what you know that counts; it's whom you know." It does matter of course what you know but it also matters whom you know. A phone call, or letter from someone a prospective employer knows, can help you land the job you want.

With luck and effort you can obtain some job interviews. When you do be sure to take plenty of time to prepare for each interview: anticipate possible questions, practice answering them, learn all you can about the job and the company or agency and arrive neatly groomed in an attractive no-nonsense outfit.

Finally take Winston Churchill's advice and, "never, never, never, never give up." You may search for several weeks before getting a job or you may not find one at all. The experience you gain and the contacts you make however will teach you a great deal and you will probably have better luck the next summer.

Chapter 22

SEMICOLONS

22a Exercise 1

Complete each sentence by adding an independent clause after the semicolon.

1. The weather is very strange; _____.
2. One of our coaches resigned; _____.
3. The birthday party was unusual; _____.
4. Eating at fast food places can lead to bad habits; _____.
5. When we are children, Christmas is magic; _____.

✓ 22b Exercise 2

Combine each of the following pairs of independent clauses into a single sentence. Use a transitional expression with the second clause, and punctuate the sentence correctly.

1. The academic standards in the school are extremely high. Most of the graduates receive scholarships to good colleges.
2. A "cruise control" is useful for a steady highway speed. You should use it only on level roads.
3. Cooking in front of television cameras can be embarrassing. I have seen cooks spill batter all over the stove, drop food on the floor, and cover up mistakes with bunches of parsley.
4. I want to get a roommate who makes up the bed. I filled out a questionnaire to help determine roommate compatibility.
5. The women's basketball team lost their first twelve games. They won the thirteenth game by one point.

22c Exercise 3

Combine each of the following pairs of independent clauses into a single sentence. Join the clauses with a coordinating conjunction and the appropriate punctuation.

1. In *I Had Trouble in Getting to Solla Sollew,* the hero, burdened by the troubles of life, goes in search of a city where people have no troubles. After many adventures, he realizes no place is trouble-free.
2. Blenders, food processors, and instant food have eliminated most slicing, dicing, and pureeing. The time required for putting together a meal seems the same.
3. Executives, managers, and employees were questioned about "flextime." All replied that the system works well.
4. In 1910 most American immigrants were Italians. In 1983 America had immigrants from 183 countries, the largest group from Mexico.
5. The story of the woman with multiple personalities shows the disease's brutal cause, bizarre symptoms, and strange development. The story is not ever sensationalized.

22a–22d Exercise 4

Complete each sentence by adding a grammatically coordinate element.

1. Tennis was once a game played by the upper classes; _____.
2. You can attend jazz festivals at the college on Sunday, June 24; on Friday, June 29; or _____.
3. Some used cars are good buys; _____.
4. Dr. Bertram Strass, a lecturer in Romance languages and literature, will speak at the meeting this week; and _____.
5. Applicants must be able to type 80 words a minute; communicate effectively, both in speech and writing; and _____.

22a–22e Exercise 5

Revise the following sentences by inserting semicolons where needed and deleting them where inappropriate.

1. Western languages contain a prejudice against left-handedness, for example, *sinister* and *gauche* are words for "left."

2.   Since 1950, the Cuban government has severely curtailed the rights of its citizens, and since 1962, the United States has imposed an economic embargo on the Castro regime.

3.   We have tickets for *La Traviata* on Tuesday, July 31, *Rigoletto* on Wednesday, August 29, and *Carmen* on Saturday, September 1.

4.   Flashing a wide grin; the applicant tried to hide his nervousness.

5.   According to a study of more than 300 adults; men cry about once a month, but women cry five times more often.

6.   The new animals in the zoo are an elephant, donated by Sri Lanka, a Bengal tiger, purchased with funds, and an aardwolf, loaned by the San Diego Zoo.

7.   Sherwood Anderson named his book of stories *The Book of the Grotesques,* however; his publisher changed the title to *Winesburg, Ohio.*

8.   Most people who use personal computers for jobs such as word processing, bookkeeping, or filing don't program their computers, instead, they buy prewritten software.

9.   The guide lists the major excavation sites around the world; where ongoing digs are uncovering secrets of ancient civilizations.

10.   "The Star-Spangled Banner" is hard to sing; but most people don't want it changed.

✓ 22a–22d Exercise 6

In the following passage, insert semicolons where necessary between items in a series and between independent clauses.

People who have trouble sleeping and people who keep odd hours have seen, I'm sure, a variety of Frankenstein films on television. The monster that started this trend took shape in Switzerland in 1816 at a gathering made up of Shelley, the poet, Mary, his future wife, and Lord Byron. To get through the wet, cold winter, the three wrote ghost stories, but the only memorable work produced was Mary's *Frankenstein.* The two famous poets wrote nothing significant, Mary, however, produced a masterpiece.

Most of the Frankenstein films that appear on television bear little resemblance to the original. The book dramatizes the horror that results when human beings assume God's creative power, but most Frankenstein films dramatize silliness. You can see such ridiculous versions as *Frankenstein and the Monster from Hell,* with the doctor running an insane asylum, *Frankenstein Conquers the World,* with an overgrown monster terrorizing Tokyo, *Frankenstein's Daughter,* with a ridiculous female robot, and *Frankenstein Meets the Space Monster,* with an interplanetary robot gone amuck.

Chapter 23

COLONS

23a–23h Exercise

To improve clarity in the following sentences, add missing colons,
remove incorrect colons, or change existing marks to colons.

1. The first electronic computer required: 17,000 vacuum tubes,
    70,000 resistors, 10,000 capacitors, and 6,000 switches.
2. Our textbook for the course is *The Americans A Social History of
    the United States, 1587–1914.*
3. He was dressed in the standard school attire corduroy slacks,
    button-down Oxford shirt, and Shetland sweater.
4. During the nineteenth century, one man stands out for the
    influence he had on other writers Emerson.
5. Dorothy L. Sayers explained the appeal of mystery novels this
    way "Death seems to provide the minds of the Anglo-Saxon race
    with a greater fund of innocent amusement than any other single
    subject ... the tale must be about dead bodies or very wicked
    people, preferably both, before the Tired Business Man can feel
    really happy."
6. Language can be ranked by its acceptability into these levels

1.	standard or formal	4.	jargon
2.	informal	5.	nonstandard
3.	slang	6.	taboo or vulgar

7. I am qualified in: COBOL, FORTRAN, and UNIX.
8. The candidates grappled over issues that especially concern
    women, equal opportunity, equal pay, abortion, old-age security.
9. The research points to a great improvement, to an immunization
    against colds.

10. The best travel guides are: Michelin, the Blue Guide, and Fodor's.
11. A single basic fact governs encoding; a computer stores only numbers.
12. They are trying to grow the following vegetables, corn, tomatoes, radishes, and broccoli.
13. These extensions of the Blue Ridge Mountains are names enshrined in American folklore, the Great Smokies, the Balsams, the Nantahalas.
14. The envelope had this notation "Attention A Human Being."
15. Sometimes a copy of a book by a living author can be a collector's item *Poems* (1934), William Golding's first book, sold recently for $4,000.

Chapter 24

DASHES, PARENTHESES, AND BRACKETS

24a–24b Exercise 1

In the following sentences, insert dashes to set off appositives and non-restrictive modifiers that contain commas.

1. The tennis instructor, a short, skinny, agile fellow, was visibly agitated by my incompetence.
2. Karl, who had recently read *The Jewel in the Crown, Gandhi,* and *The Blood Seed,* claimed to be an expert on India.
3. Blacks, Jews, Catholics, southerners, women, people of minority groups are sought out for political endorsements.
4. The editorial, which attacked university policies on housing, meal tickets, and zoning regulations, was written by a freshman.
5. The book contains reminiscences by a wide range of people, journalists, musicians, artists, critics, and teachers.

24c–24d Exercise 2

To emphasize elements and to set off interrupters, insert dashes or change existing marks to dashes.

1. Human beings, of whom there are today close to five billion, rely primarily on plants for food.
2. On the Fourth of July we had fireworks, not sparklers or Roman candles, but a large professional extravaganza.
3. Just below Lee Highway, parallel to it, in fact, is Arlington Boulevard.

4. He was, it was now unmistakably clear, a coward.
5. The subway travelers have a high tolerance level for trash, dirt, and graffiti (or they have no alternative transportation).
6. "He's, oh, my heavens, he's already here."
7. Finally (I think it was in October, or maybe November) he went to see a doctor.
8. Eakins' portraits are honest, honest in the external details and honest in the psychological characterization.
9. The riddle was a conundrum, that is, a riddle that depends on a pun.
10. The article was about America's biggest business, food.

24e–24f Exercise 3

Use parentheses to add at an appropriate place the information specified for each sentence.

EXAMPLE: The new mapmaking technique for the oceans has uncovered previously unknown seamounts. [Explain that seamounts are underwater volcanoes.] → The new mapmaking technique for the oceans has uncovered previously unknown seamounts (underwater volcanoes).

1. Generally, two-way or three-way speakers will sound better than single-cone. [Explain that two-way is coaxial; three-way, triaxial.]
2. T. E. Lawrence published an account of his World War I adventures in *The Seven Pillars of Wisdom.* [Add that the account was published in 1926.]
3. VLSI research is helping speed up the evolution of microprocessors. [Explain that VLSI means "Very Large-Scale Integration."]
4. The few players who engage in serious tournament chess are mainly concerned with strategy. [Instruct readers to refer to Chapter 16.]
5. The exhibit at the Anacostia Neighborhood Museum is *Black Wings,* about black American aviators. [Add the dates July 2–August 5.]
6. New York City, which is surrounded by major tomato-growing regions, depends mainly on California and Mexico for its tomatoes. [Explain that the regions are New Jersey, Long Island, and upstate New York.]

7. The goldsmith said that for $4,200 he could design the trophy. [Add the comment "That's not a bad price."]
8. I am an admirer of the work of Leonard. [Add the comment "More accurately, I am a fan."]

24g–24h Exercise 4

Use brackets to add the explanations and insertions specified for each sentence.

1. According to the explanation, "Teletext magazines consist of 100 to 5,000 "frames' of graphics and information." [Explain in the previous quote that "frames" means the same thing as "video screens."]
2. Sir Herbert Read wrote of "the no-man's-years between the wars." [Indicate that these "years" are 1919–1939.]
3. According to the newspaper, "The police and 'volunter' auxiliaries surrounded the statehouse and checked identifications and otherwise harassed the protesters." [Show that it was the newspaper that misspelled volunteer.]
4. According to Bruce Catton, "This four-year tragedy ... is the *Hamlet* and *King Lear* of the American past." [Indicate that by "tragedy" Catton means the Civil War.]
5. About a possible operation her father needed, Virginia Woolf wrote in a letter that "any operation however slight ... must be bad when you'r old." [Show that it was Virginia Woolf who misspelled *you're*.]

Chapter 25

PERIODS, QUESTION MARKS, AND EXCLAMATION POINTS

25a–25c Exercise 1

Revise the following sentences so that the periods are used correctly.

1. The tourists always ask when they can see the ghosts that haunt the castle?
2. She said calmly, "Sorry, I didn't mean to upset you."
3. Garden flowers fall into three categories:
    1. annuals.
    2. biennials.
    3. perennials
4. Chinese art was flourishing by the time of the Shang dynasty, about 1500 B.C. to 1028 B.C.
5. Would you please send a transcript of my grades to the address listed below?

25d–25e Exercise 2

Revise the sentences so that question marks are used correctly both at the ends of sentences and within sentences to show emphasis or doubt.

1. What does rattlesnake taste like.
2. Is the telephone company our servant, our partner, our master, or merely off the hook.
3. The founding fathers did believe in separation of church and state, didn't they.

4. The Trojan War (in the 1200s B.C.) was fought between Greece and the city of Troy. [Indicate that the date of the war is doubtful.]

5. How can we make retirees feel productive is not adequately discussed.

25h Exercise 3

Improve the following sentences by eliminating exclamation points. Replace vague words with specific details or add words and phrases that express the importance of the ideas.

1. The party was fabulous!

2. The paper should be a five-page discussion of American transcendentalism. It must have a thesis supported by concrete details!

3. We must take steps to conserve energy!

4. Last Saturday's game was the greatest I have ever seen!

5. After spending hours at registration, I finally managed to get a perfect schedule!

Chapter 26

APOSTROPHES

26a Exercise 1

In the following sentences, change each underlined phrase to a comparable possessive containing an apostrophe.

EXAMPLE: The border guard examined the visa of every tourist. →
             The border guard examined every tourist's visa.

1. The face of Medusa turned people to stone.
2. The waterfront of San Francisco attracts many visitors.
3. The weather can affect the emotions of anyone.
4. He lost his pay for a whole week.
5. The seismograph measured the intensity of the earthquakes.
6. People have always been fascinated by the love affair of Antony and Cleopatra.
7. The dressing rooms of the singers and the dancers were beneath the stage.
8. The press attacked the policy of the secretary of state.
9. One of the discoveries of Archimedes was the principle of buoyancy.
10. The new shop specializes in games for children.
11. The book by James Fallows is about Japan.
12. The schools in both cities lack adequate funds.
13. A hog belonging to our neighbors was killed in the tornado.
14. The meaning of the hieroglyphics was deciphered in 1822.
15. The landscape in Kansas is an expanse of tall grass.

26a Exercise 2

Insert apostrophes where necessary to indicate possessive nouns.

Hibernation is a general term describing an animals sleeplike state during particular times of the day or year. "True" hibernation occurs only in warm-blooded animals that hibernate to avoid winters harsh temperatures and reduce the need for food. The ground squirrel, for example, is a true hibernator. In winter, the squirrels body temperature falls close to that of the surrounding air and its heartbeat is extremely slow. The true hibernators sleep, however, is not very deep; the animal is only napping and can rouse itself whenever it chooses. Other kinds of hibernation include the butterflys cocoon state, the bats daytime sleep, the hummingbirds night trance, and the desert snakes dormancy when water is scarce.

26a–26d Exercise 3

Edit the following passage for incorrect or missing apostrophes.

I edited my manuscript about Democratic conventions during the 1960s with the help of a software program named Grammatik, who's purpose is to point out possible grammatical and punctuation errors. Grammatik even makes suggestion's for correcting these errors. Its a very effective program; it doesn't overlook much. It found two *ms* in *ommitted,* a missing apostrophe in *didnt,* an unnecessary apostrophe in *her's,* several unnecessary commas, and about seven examples of wordiness. It also pointed out that I had used in the text fifteen *verys* and ten *howevers.* Grammatiks skills improved the accuracy of the paper. It's thorough checking surprised me. Now that Ive improve the manuscripts grammar, punctuation, and style, I need a software program to help with the content.

Chapter 27

QUOTATION MARKS AND ELLIPSIS MARKS

27a–27b Exercise 1

Correct any quotation marks that are positioned incorrectly in relation to other marks of punctuation.

1. In none of the many novels and stories about Sherlock Holmes did he once say, "Elementary, my dear Watson".

2. Over 100 years ago, Chief Sealth of the Duwamish tribe said, "The White man must treat the beasts of this land as his brothers. What is man without the beasts?"

3. In Faulkner's story "The Bear", the hunted animal, when fatally wounded "fell all of a piece, as a tree falls."

4. How did the instruction manual say to answer the question "Is this to be installed on an MP/M system?"

5. The teacher shouted to the now intimidated student, "You cannot have forgotten the entire multiplication table!"

6. I lay awake all night wondering, "Before that enormous crowd, will remember all the words of 'The Star-Spangled Banner'?"

7. It is redundant to write "from whence"; *whence* means "from where."

8. According tot he author, Caesar was "a nobleman of surpassing prestige and authority (Kahn 56)."

9. Langston Hughes wrote about the nature of the blues: "The music is behind it that seems to say, 'In spite of fate, bad luck, these blues themselves, I'm going on!'"

10. According to the guide, "The preposition *in* means 'located or being with,' but it also quite correctly means 'moving or directed inside': for example, *going in the house* or *dived in the water*."

27a–27b Exercise 2

Incorporate the original statement into sentences according to the instructions.

Statement: In dealing with the future . . . it is more important to be imaginative and insightful than to be one hundred percent "right." (Alvin Toffler, *Future Shock*)

1. Quote the entire statement, placing "according to Alvin Toffler" at the beginning.
2. Quote the entire statement, placing "Alvin Toffler wrote in *Future Shock*" at the end.
3. Quote the entire statement, inserting "Alvin Toffler has written" after *future* and before *it*.
4. Quote the entire statement, placing "Was it Alvin Toffler who wrote" at the beginning.
5. Paraphrase all of the statement, making it into an indirect quote. Give credit to Toffler.

27d Exercise 3

Insert quotation marks wherever necessary in the following sentences.

1. The Haunted and the Haunters is a spine-tingling ghost story.
2. One of Ogden Nash's poems is titled At Least I'm Not the King of Fool Who Sobs, What Kind of Fool Am I?
3. On Muzak, Johnny Mathis was singing Winter Wonderland.
4. The essay entitled The Blues: A Poetic Form analyzed the music of twelve blues singers.
5. In the *Washington Post* Friday, the editorial, Federal Officials Shirk Duty, was particularly critical of Congress.

27e Exercise 4

Explain the reasons for the quotation marks in the following sentences.

1. On the Scrabble board, the tiles spelled out "SCOWLS," "SOBS," and "POOLS."
2. The dump calls itself a "restaurant" and the mush it serves "food."
3. The child cannot pronounce "aluminum."

4. The artist was "discovered" when he was fifty years old.
5. His only "exercise" is opening and closing the refrigerator door.
6. The advertisement maintains that the film is "art."

27a–27f Exercise 5

Correct any errors made in the use of quotation marks.

1. The first novel Mark Twain wrote was "The Adventures of Thomas Jefferson Snodgrass."
2. In Liverpool, a cat is a moggy.
3. The editorial, A Step Toward Success, says that the program is "an investment in future security;" however, I am not sure the program is that valuable.
4. The line "In my beginning is my end" appears in the poem *East Coker* from the book "Four Quarters".
5. Have you ever heard of a turtle called a "cooter?"
6. According to Edith Hamilton, Greek mythology developed when "little distinction had been made . . . between the real and unreal".
7. Was the actor in the right place on the stage when he said, "What's here? a cup, clos'd in my true love's hand?"
8. "Don't touch the"—it was too late.
9. "Duke" Wayne had his best role when he played "Rooster" Cogburn in "True Grit."
10. Victory is "just around the corner" and "almost in our grasp."

27g Exercise 6

Use ellipsis marks to show the omissions indicated.

1. According to H. L. Mencken, "To be in love is merely to be in a state of perceptual anaesthesia—to mistake an ordinary young man for a Greek god or an ordinary young woman for a goddess." [Omit all of the sentence after "anaesthesia."]

2. Edith Hamilton has written: "Five hundred years before Christ in a little town on the far western border of the settled and civilized world, a strange new power was at work. Something had awakened in the minds and spirits of the men there which was so to influence the world that the slow passage of long time, of century

upon century and the shattering changes they brought, would be
powerless to wear away that deep impress. Athens had entered
upon her brief and magnificent flowering of genius which so
molded the world of mind and spirit that our mind and spirit
today are different." [Omit the second sentence.]

3.   Leslie Fiedler writes of Faulkner's writings: "The detective story is
the inevitable crown of Faulkner's work; in it (the stories in
Knight's Gambit and *Intruder in the Dust*) many strains of his
writing find fulfillment, not least his commitment to the
'switcheroo' and the surprise ending." [Omit the part of the quotation in parentheses.]

4.   In "The Second Coming" Yeats writes:

Turning and turning in the widening gyre
The falcon cannot hear the falconer;
Things fall apart; the centre cannot hold;
Mere anarchy is loosed upon the world,
The blood-dimmed tide is loosed, and everywhere
The ceremony of innocence is drowned;
The best lack all conviction, while the worst
Are full of passionate intensity. [Omit lines 4, 5, and 6.]

5.   At 5:30 Mountain War Time, when the Atomic Age began, "At that
great moment in history, ranking with the moment in the long ago
when man first put fire to work for him and started on his march
to civilization, the vast energy locked within the hearts of the
atoms of matter was released for the first time in a burst of flame
such as had never before been seen on this planet." [Omit the
beginning of the quote through "civilization."]

Chapter 28

ITALICS/UNDERLINING

28a–28f Exercise

Underline any words that should be italicized.

1. The Statue of Liberty, a book by Marvin Trachtenberg, tells the fascinating story of Bartholdi's efforts to "glorify ... Liberty."
2. Lewis and Clark brought back from their western expedition the Columbian lily (Fritillaria pudica).
3. The child kept throwing rocks into the lake—kerplunk, kerplunk, kerplunk.
4. Many people object to using the masculine pronoun he to refer to both sexes.
5. He was wearing a trenchcoat straight out of Casablanca.
6. Lequesne pronounced the finished statue his chef d'oeuvre.
7. Chess was his only love. [emphasis on *only*]
8. Stamma labeled the vertical rows of the chess board from a to h.
9. Some newspapers use pontiff as a synonym for pope.
10. Watteau's The Embarkation for Cythera is filled with angels and happy, elegant people.
11. She is supposed to be a femme fatale in The Young and the Restless.
12. Civilization has made some progress. [emphasis on *has*]
13. The word check is abbreviated + in algebraic notation.
14. Toe shoes were first used in the ballet La Sylphide.
15. On the program were Mozart's Jupiter Symphony and Rachmaninoff's Prelude in G Minor.

Chapter 29

HYPHENS AND SLASHES

29a Exercise 1

Should the following compounds be hyphenated, fused into one word, or left as two separate words?

1. machine gun (verb)
2. machine gun (noun)
3. drop off (verb)
4. drop off (noun)
5. field test (verb)
6. field test (noun)
7. eye opener (noun)
8. eye lash (noun)
9. light year (noun)
10. light plane (noun)

29a–29d Exercise 2

Supply any missing hyphens in the following passage.

Many people, enjoying the resurgence of a 4,500 year old game, are kicking around a golfball size object. Although kickball games have long been popular, a new version was invented by John Stalberger of Portland, Oregon. In order to rehabilitate a badly injured knee, he gave soccer style kicks to a mini size ball. After Stalberger introduced his "footbag" to people at a state fair, the game grew in popularity. Two companies, which started producing the footbag, got in a patent controversy but made an out of court settlement. The companies' products are somewhat different. One markets a four paneled footbag; the other, a two piece version. Other companies now have similar products—one an eight dollar fire engine red bag with a devil logo. Now there are even championships in which contestants play a sort of tennis and a sort of volleyball game over a 5 foot high net.

29f–29i Exercise 3

Wherever possible, substitute slashes in alternatives, combinations, or fractions. Assume that the context for these sentences is informal or technical.

1. The agency will provide car or bus transportation to the site of the ceremony.
2. WXTR AM or FM will have regular progress reports from the football coaches.
3. Interest rates have gone up three-tenths of a percent.
4. The Biloxi and Gulfport area is one of the fastest growing areas on the Gulf Coast.
5. If a person writes a company about a billing error, the company must acknowledge his or her letter within thirty days.

Chapter 30

ABBREVIATIONS AND NUMBERS

30a–30b Exercise 1

Make any necessary corrections in the use of abbreviations.

1. The oldest house in town is at 120 W. Harbor Street.
2. My uncle used to tell stories about his war buddy, Sgt. Dumcke.
3. Miss. Ramsey was the most feared teacher in our grammar school.
4. The board elected James Ogden, Senior, as its president.
5. His case was heard by the Hon. Lucille Godbold.
6. The textile workers have launched an advertising campaign featuring products made in the U.S.
7. The Romans invaded Britain in B.C. 55 and again in 43 A.D.
8. The first lecturer will be Dr. Charles Shields, Ph. D.

30a–30b Exercise 2

Eliminate any inappropriate abbreviations in the following passage.

The Germans used submarines, called U-boats, to enforce a naval blockade of Eng. in the Atl. The U.S. had to keep the sea lanes open for supplies and for a possible invasion. The German submarines, traveling in "wolf packs," moved to the American East Coast On Jan. 12, 1942, they opened an offensive off Cape Cod, MA, and soon after inflicted heavy destruction from Canada to Jacksonville, FL. From Jan.–Apr. 1942, almost 200 ships were sunk. Then Adm. Doenitz, the German commander, moved farther south and torpedoed 182 ships in May and June. Adm. King organized small escort vessels into an interlocking convoy system to combat the Germans. The convoy system, well-equipped destroyers, and radar-equipped planes eventually controlled the menace.

30c–30e Exercise 3

Revise the following passages so that numbers are expressed appropriately.

1. Although the first guns with revolving cylinders had been made three hundred years earlier, Sam Colt got an American patent in eighteen thirty-five. Colt was a good businessman as well as an inventor. For example, in the Seminole Indian War, he sold officers all the five-shot Colt pistols that he had and fifty eight-shot rifles. Colt then developed the six-shot gun and established a factory with a production line. By eighteen fifty-seven, his factory was producing two hundred and fifty pistols a day.

2. Jane Hook is indeed a prolific mystery novelist. She has written 5 novels in the last 4 years, 3 of the mysteries are set in a hospital— a good background since Hook was for 15 years a hospital administrator. The other 2 novels also touch on real experiences; 1 is built around a psychiatric symposium, and the other has a 36-year-old nurse as the protagonist. The novels tend to be longer than the average mystery. The shortest of the 5 is 255 pages, and the longest is 420 pages.

Chapter 31

CAPITAL LETTERS

31a–31h Exercise

In the following sentences, correct any incorrect capitalization.

1. As early as 1500, the English Bulldog was bred to bait bulls.
2. The president attacked the "demagoguery" of the speech made by the Communist speaker.
3. A Federal indictment was issued by U.S. attorney J. Frederick Motz.
4. The Bulgarian Government was accused of condoning drug trafficking.
5. A majority of republicans joined the democrats in support of a resolution sponsored by a senator from Maine.
6. The Commission recommended that High School students study English, Math, Science, Computer Science, and Foreign Languages.
7. The east–west conflict was aggravated by the unexpected announcement of increased Military spending.
8. Husbands and Wives may file a Tax Return jointly.
9. This Summer, the Chester public library announced that three Personal Computers could be checked out and taken home.
10. A pamphlet entitled "Life Insurance: Facts You Need to Know" explains the three basic types of Life Insurance policies.
11. The chief psychoactive ingredient in Marijuana (*Cannabis Sativa*) is delta-9-tetrahydrocannabinol, or thc.
12. Silver coins have gradually disappeared; during the Winter of 1970, the Government removed all silver from the Half Dollar.
13. The St. Lawrence seaway extends from the Atlantic ocean to the Western end of Lake Superior and allows ocean carriers to enter the midwest.

14. In the first Moon landing, Armstrong and Aldrin collected 48.5 Lbs. of rock and soil.

15. Have you seen *Go Tell It on the Mountain,* a tv adaptation of James Baldwin's Novel?

16. The Association has registered 661 varieties of trees; a holly is the smallest, and a sequoia is the largest.

17. "To make his magic fiction, look real," Nabokov has said, "The artist sometimes places it ... within a definite, specific historical frame."

18. For lunch we ate chicken cooked in a Dutch oven, French fries, and a salad with Russian dressing.

19. The constitution provided for a census every ten years to determine the number of Representatives who would go to congress from each state.

20. "Beauty: a Combination From Sappho" is a translation by Rossetti of a lyric composed in the sixth century b.c.

PART III: REVIEW EXERCISES

Correct the punctuation and mechanics in the following passages.

1. Horror films long a popular genre explore the supernatural the inexplicable and the evil all to terrify viewers relentlessly. The first attempts at provoking fear were not true horror films all the mystery was logically explained at the finish. In three classic films however no rational explanation is offered or even can be.

    In 1930 Universal studios made a film about a blood drinking count, who could return from the dead Dracula. In this film directed by Tod Browning vampires travel the globe the dead live the innocent die and the irrational seems real. Audiences can find little comfort even a stake through Draculas heart cannot stop the malignant forces.

    The next important horror film was directed by James Whale a british stage director. This film Frankenstein became a classic with it's brilliant performance by Boris Karloff as it's horrifying but tragic monster. The plot of the film 1931 is familiar. The brilliant Dr. Frankenstein succeeds in creating a living creature out of piece's of the dead. After killing the doctors assistant the monster escapes from the castle. Like Dracula this monster kills the innocent, and has been resurrected periodically in sequels.

    The only other horror films that have ever rivaled Dracula and Frankenstein in importance are the films about Wolf Man. Introduced to the screen by Henry Hull the first werewolf film was The Werewolf of London 1934. The figure of a werewolf or lycantrope derived from the legends of central Europe where people had long heard tales of a man who changed to a wolf at every full moon, and stalked and killed victims through the night. In the future we will probably continue to see films containing these classic horror film monsters who's mysterious illogical existence continues to fascinate us.

2. When Columbus landed in Cuba the natives told him about "a sort of grain called maiz." In the New World corn, or maize, had long been a staple crop. And it still is. Today the U.S.s per capita consumption of corn or food derived from corn is more than 3 lbs a

day and the U.S. grows so much corn it can export a 3rd of the crop. Corn has been an extremely reliable crop no famine has ever decimated the U.S. as wheat and potato famines have decimated other country's.

As a food corn lends itself to wide variety. When Cortes entered Mexico in 1519 tortillas formed the basis of the Mexican diet. South Americans also prepared tamales, the equivalent of the european meat pie and chinese spring roll. Early American settlers survived partly on hominy grits succotash and cornpone all derived from corn. It was even possible to make maize beer but this drink was never as popular in America as it was in Peru and Brazil. somewhat later the richer American People could afford wheat the poorer ones ate a lot of cornmeal mush and johnnycakes.

Today we still eat all these ancient dishes, however in addition we depend heavily on meat, that comes from animals nourished by corn. We drink whiskey, made from fermented corn. And we use corn oil cornstarch and corn sweetener in innumerable products.

PART IV

Style

Chapter 32

WORD CHOICE

32a Exercise 1

Revise the following passages to make the formality of the vocabulary consistent.

1. There are few aficionados of checkers. Most people think of checkers as a game for small fry. But this game can bring jollity and challenge even to the intelligentsia. Players can toil for years trying to divine the moves and can cram from hundreds of tomes that contain the lore of checkers masters. The competition at times gets fierce; it's no place for sissies with butterflies. One game played by virtuosos lasted seven hours and thirty minutes only to end in a draw.

2. You'll love the yummy cuisine you find all over New Orleans—especially the seafood. The oysters in an elegant café like Antoine's can be the pièce de résistance of a lavish supper—something that will really fill the bill. Whenever you're looking for a bellyful of sumptuous chow, you might consider the trout Véronique at the Hotel Pontchartrain or the shrimp rémoulade at Arnaud's.

32b (1) Exercise 2

Consider the following pairs of words. How do the connotations of each differ? In other words, what emotional responses do you associate with each?

1. curious/nosey
2. skinny/thin
3. melody/tune
4. chauffeur/driver
5. fiddle/violin
6. movie/film
7. orchestra/band
8. mob/crowd
9. dine/eat
10. lawn/yard
11. cuisine/food
12. attire/clothes

32b (1) Exercise 3

Discuss the effect that each word in the parentheses would have on the sentence as a whole.

1. As the kayak rushed uncontrollably through the white water, I felt as if I were being (thrown, rocketed, cast, hurled) into space.
2. The fans (swarmed, flocked, gathered, thronged) around the winning baseball players.
3. To escape to a more exciting world, Tom reads only spy (books, novels, thrillers, adventures).
4. The initial deposit can be as low as $250, and depositors earn market rates on all balances no matter how (tiny, little, small, puny).
5. Someone had hurriedly (written, printed, lettered, scrawled) "wash me" in the dust (enshrouding, covering, blanketing, coating) the truck.

32b (1) Exercise 4

Change any words that are inappropriate to the context because of their connotations.

If you are toiling to become fit, you can try several schemes to lost poundage and to gain robustness. First, limit the time you spend ogling TV or availing yourself of video games. Whenever feasible, get out of the house and frolic, walk, or jog. Second, avoid sumptuous repasts. Eat plenty of legumes and fruit. Little food and lots of exercise will give birth to results.

32b (2) Exercise 5

Rewrite the following passages to make the generalities more specific whenever appropriate. You may invent any specific details necessary to enliven the prose.

1. One incident involved a student found carrying a deadly weapon on the school premises. The problem was handled by the proper authorities, who expelled the student and referred him to a court. The person in charge of the occurrence said that the learning environment could not tolerate such dangerous behavior and that

the perpetrator should be rehabilitated, not just punished by removal from the scene.

2. The team was ranked high in the polls early in the year. As the season began, the team started off by losing several games. Evidently, those working with the players did not do a good job. The players had problems that were not solved by any of the measures taken. The team continued to lose, and at the end of the disastrous season, the staff made plans to improve the situation next year.

32b (3) Exercise 6

Pick five of the following abstractions and supply a concrete representation.

EXAMPLES: terrorism → the hijacking of the *Achille Lauro*
restraint → refusing a chocolate eclair because of a diet

1. fright
2. pollution
3. ambition
4. poverty
5. optimism
6. relaxation
7. power
8. invigoration
9. speed
10. difficulty

32c (1) Exercise 7

In the following passages, strings of clichés create a dull and lifeless style. Rewrite the passages so that they have energy and meaning.

1. A good friend is always tried and true, ready and willing to help in time of need. Whether you need a helping hand or just a pat on the back, a real friend will provide. If you get into serious trouble, false friends will drop you like a hot potato. But a real friend will stick by your side. A good friend is one in a million.

2. The ball was snapped into the hands of the eagerly awaiting quarterback, who then handed off quick as a wink to the halfback. Like greased lightning, the halfback sprang through a gaping hole in the line. Lo and behold, this brilliant performance was cut off in midstream by fate in the form of a tackler big as all outdoors. The ball popped loose into the waiting hands of an offensive

lineman who lumbered 20 yards into the end zone, thus snatching victory from the jaws of defeat.

32c (2) Exercise 8

Identify the euphemisms in the following passage. When you think they are deceptive or pretentious, make substitutions.

When your beloved lifetime companion, having passed through the golden years, reaches the time to pass onward to the final resting place, consider the facilities of the Bow Wow Perpetual Interment Memorial Garden. We offer the full gamut of prearrangement option plans for such eventualities. A ceremoniously frocked mortician will deliver individualized obsequies for each doggie you lose. Come visit the resting places and slumber chambers for your dear beloved departed companions.

32d (1) Exercise 9

Identify the gobbledygook in the following passage and rewrite in plain English.

It has been shown at this point in time that contributions to the community improvement fund have fallen short of expectations. We had envisionized reaching our goal during the course of our fund-raising drive to accumulate the optimum number of contributions. Even though we utilized all feasible resources subsequent to the initiation of the drive, the requisite amount of money has not materialized, and we find ourselves with a deficit of considerable magnitude. It is clear that a plan of action must be activated that will minimize our problems. We must be cognizant of improved techniques that can expedite our endeavors in the future.

32d (2) Exercise 10

Remove the surplus words from the following passage.

I read the other day that in actual fact 47 percent of American adults cannot swim. The final outcome of not being able to swim could be drowning. Each and every year thousands of people drown. In my personal opinion, teaching their children to swim should be a first priority of all parents. The effort would be small in size compared with the end result—protection from drowning. Also, by means of being able to swim, any and all people can enjoy different varieties of water sports like surfing and scuba diving. Since the benefits range all the way from safety to pleasure, the ability to swim is absolutely essential.

32d (3) Exercise 11

Clarify the following dense noun phrases by using hyphens or by rewriting.

1. book sales conference
2. former patient payment plan
3. baboon heart transplant
4. last chapter conclusions
5. high school student fitness program

32e Exercise 12

Find terms that might replace the following words and phrases.

1. Latino
2. cripple
3. old man and old lady
4. the working man
5. policeman

32e Exercise 13

Examine the following sets of terms and discuss how you think people might react to them. Would an audience find them acceptable, unacceptable, current, or unfashionable? Would different audiences react differently?

1. black, Afro-American, African-American, Negro
2. Native American, American Indian, Amerind, Abo-American (Aboriginal-American)

3. handicapped, physically impaired, physically challenged
4. WASP, Caucasian, white, Anglo
5. poor students, exceptional students
6. drunks, alcoholics, people whit alcohol dependency

32e   Exercise 14

Without using compounds (*she or he, him or her*), eliminate the discriminatory nouns and pronouns from the following passage.

Sales brochures can be of great value to a salesman. They are useful for distribution to potential customers who ask him about his company or its products. If the brochure looks professional and sophisticated, the salesman can give it to one of the girls at the front desk to ensure that he will get to see the right man in the company.

32e   Exercise 15

Would the blanks in the following sentences be more typically filled with *he* or with *she*?

1. _____ needs a raise to help support a family.
2. _____ does not need a raise because _____ is married and has additional income.
3. _____ is very attractive—competent, tough, decisive.
4. _____ is very attractive—diplomatic, polite, adaptable.
5. _____ is getting married; _____ will no longer be dependable.
6. _____ is getting married; _____ will now be more settled.
7. _____ is not in at the moment; _____ is probably at a meeting.
8. _____ is not in at the moment; _____ is probably taking a break.
9. If _____ is not at home on Saturday night, _____ is likely to be out drinking beer.
10. If _____ is not at home on Saturday night, _____ is likely to be at a concert.

Chapter 33

SENTENCE STYLE

33a (1)–33a (2) Exercise 1

By applying the techniques discussed in 33a (1) and 33a (2), combine each of the following into a single sentence.

1. Some species of fish live many years in captivity. Others die in a year or so, either of old age or unknown causes.
2. A serious athlete must maintain a strict physical regimen. He or she must also maintain a strict mental discipline.
3. Apathy pervades this campus. Only a fraction of the student body votes in any election.
4. Reading a good daily newspaper will help you stay informed. Reading a good weekly news magazine will help you stay informed.
5. Honey Island Swamp once served as a hideout for pirates and bandits. The swamp was also a hideout for bootleggers and their whiskey stills.
6. The flowers have vanished. The tourists have vanished.
7. The boat circled back. It dropped anchor.
8. Technically, the term "shin splints" refers to pain along the lower, inner part of the leg. The term is often used to refer to any leg pain resulting from overuse.
9. Fireworks produce colorful displays of light and sound. Firecrackers produce monotonous noise.
10. The model ships were not just matchsticks glued together. They were tiny, ornate, meticulous creations.
11. The teacher calls on us to state the facts we have learned. We are also supposed to explain their significance.
12. His eyes began to adjust to the dark. he could see a shape emerging from the trees.

13. Shakespeare created heroes with flaws. He also created villains with consciences.
14. At some point, everyone yearns for second chance. Few ever get one.
15. Nero could not have fiddled while Rome burned. Fiddles had not been invented.

33a (3)–33a (6) Exercise 2

Using some of the suggested subordinating techniques, combine each of the passages into a single sentence, eliminating choppy prose and vague pronoun reference.

1. The bird-watchers all had binoculars hanging from their necks. The bird-watchers climbed hills and splashed through the swamps in search of the black-throated green warbler.
2. Lincoln rode into Springfield on April 15, 1837. He carried all he owned in his saddlebags.
3. Gardeners can buy software. This supplies such information as when, where, and what to plant in particular areas.
4. Nellie Bly once pretended to be insane. She had had herslef committed to a mental hospital. Her purpose was to study conditions.
5. Advancement seemed to rest on flattering the executives. This was a policy designed to promote hypocrisy.
6. The woman died. She left her house and her money to her dog Teddy.
7. The five students were selling drugs. They were expelled from school.
8. A patient's mental attitude affects the chances for recovery. We cannot be sure that a good attitude will always effect a cure.
9. Da Vinci is recognized as one of the most versatile geniuses in history. He was a painter, a geologist, an astronomer, an inventor, a botanist, and a student of human anatomy.
10. The rock 'n' roll of the Tail Gators is often called "swampy." This refers to the warm and relaxed feeling of blues and folk music.
11. A red flag cannot anger a bull. Bulls are colorblind.
12. The man was brought to court. He claimed that someone had slipped a mysterious drug into his drink.

13. The stolen car was returned. Its owner found a note that said, "The brakes need attention."

14. Halloween used to be fun. It was ruined by the poisoned fudge and the needles in apples.

15. The Heimlich maneuver can be used on young people. Special care must be taken in using it on babies.

33a Exercise 3

Improve the prose of the following passages by using the techniques for coordinating and subordinating previously discussed. With each passage, try several different ways of combining to achieve the most satisfactory results.

1. The dinosaurs may have died out because the earth was hit by a huge asteroid. The impact of the asteroid threw dust into the atmosphere. There was enough dust to block sunlight from the earth's surface. Then plant life was killed. Then the dinosaurs starved to death.

2. Many employers will not hire people without work experience. Perhaps employers should have apprentice programs. In apprentice programs, people could work part time. And they could work for lower pay than other workers. The apprentice program could count as job experience. The program could improve chances for employment.

3. George Bryan "Beau" Brummell inherited a moderate estate from his father. He set up lavish bachelor quarters in London. While he was in London, he influenced the style of men's clothing and manners for almost twenty years. Gambling and extravagant living bankrupted him. He fled to France to escape creditors in 1816. He was jailed for debt in France in 1835. He died in France in a mental institution.

4. During the seventeenth century many people were put to death. These people were accused of being witches. They were blamed for everything. They were blamed for bad weather, bad crops, diseases, and deaths. In England, Matthew Hopkins was a famous witch hunter. He called himself the "Witch Finder General." He claimed to have a list of witches. The list was given to him by the Devil. He and his aides went from town to town. They were searching for witches. They charged the townspeople money. Witch hunting was very profitable. Hopkins maintained that suspected witches should take the "swimming test." In the "swimming test" the suspects were thrown into ponds or rivers. Floaters were judged to be witches. They were put to death. Sinkers were presumed innocent. By that time, though, they had probably already drowned.

33a Exercise 4

Improve the following passage by rearranging and rewriting to vary sentence beginnings.

I have gotten together with about a dozen friends every New Year's Day for the past few years. Our day begins with a lunch of ham and black-eyed peas, the traditional symbols of good luck for the coming year. We watch the college bowl games on television then from afternoon until night. We switch to pizza and old movies after the games are over. Our day finally ends with a familiar ritual. We write down our New Year's resolutions in a faded, old notebook; date them; and sign them. Someone in the group then turns to the beginning of the notebook and reads through all our past years' resolutions. We laugh and groan over our triumphs and failures. The new year seems to begin when I share with my friends this moment between the past and the future.

33b (1) Exercise 5

Rewrite these loose sentences as periodic.

1. She finally won a beauty contest after years of practice and coaching, after rigorous diets and plastic surgery, after countless attempts that ended in defeat.
2. The reality of our loss hit us when the dawn revealed the damage, when we found a burned shell instead of a house.
3. I entered a singing contest once in the sixth grade, although I cannot imagine why, since I could barely carry a tune.
4. Just give me an A rather than encouragement, advice, and study aids.

5. The star swept into the room wrapped in furs, signing autographs, posing for photographs, followed by a throng of admirers.

33b (2) Exercise 6

Make the loose sentences cumulative by adding structures onto each. If the beginnings do not stimulate ideas, substitute a few of your own.

EXAMPLE: The man was dressed like a gypsy. → The man was dressed like a gypsy, in a red silk shirt open to the waist, tight black pants, a bandanna on his head, gold loops in his ears, and a tight cummerbund circling his waist.

1. My favorite memories from childhood are summer afternoons.
2. The hamburger tasted like plastic.
3. My grammar school principal seemed frightening.
4. He wanted a wife who was like his mother.
5. I thought that college life would be fun.

33b (3) Exercise 7

Combine each of the following sets of sentences into one sentence with a climactic order.

1. On the camping trip, our tent washed away in a flash flood. Also, the mosquitoes attacked us in swarms. The heat was unbearable. Our food spoiled.
2. The interviewer asked me what jobs I had held previously. She asked me if I were free for dinner. She asked me what salary I expected. She asked me what degree I held.
3. To prove he was as good a cook as my mother, my father prepared an elaborate dinner. He made Caesar salad. He concocted a flaming dessert which caught the tablecloth on fire. He fixed pork chops stuffed with raising dressing.
4. Success is a matter of priorities. You must decide what you are willing to give up to attain your goals. You decide which goals are important to your success. You must decide what you consider success to be.
5. The child sat on Santa's lap. She pulled on his beard. She asked him for about a thousand dollars worth of toys. She said crossly, "You ain't my daddy." She stared at him hostilely.

33b (4) Exercise 8

Revise the following sentences to create balanced structures by repeating structure and, where possible, key vocabulary.

EXAMPLE: Although the plot of the mystery is ordinary, the book has unusual characters. → The plot of the mystery is ordinary, but the characters are extraordinary.

1. He knew when to give in. In addition, he also understood when he should give up.
2. Although he was friendly and outgoing in public, in private he was hostile as well as withdrawn.
3. The cost of one episode of *Miami Vice* was $1,500,000. The budget was $1,167,000 for running the entire Miami vice squad for a whole year.
4. To young people, the absence of pleasure is painful. The lack of pain, when people get older, is a pleasure.
5. Some people say that the clothes make the man. In my opinion, however, the man can have a beneficial effect on the clothes.

33b Exercise 9

Determine whether the following sentences are periodic, cumulative, climactic, or balanced.

1. Integrity without knowledge is weak and useless, and knowledge without integrity is dangerous and dreadful. (Samuel Johnson)

2. There are, indeed, many other jobs that are unpleasant, and yet no one thinks of abolishing them—that of the plumber, that of the soldier, that of the garbage-man, that of the priest hearing confessions, that of the sand-hog, and so on. (H. L. Mencken)

3. Yet because the moth was so small, and so simple a form of the energy that was rolling in at the open window and driving its way through so many narrow and intriguing corridors in my own brain and in those of other human beings, there was something marvelous as well as pathetic about him. (Virginia Woolf)

4. The golf gallery is the Punchinello of the great sports mob, the clown crowd, an uncontrollable, galloping, galumphing horde, that wanders hysterically over manicured pasture acreage of an

afternoon, clucking to itself, trying to keep quiet, making funny noises, sweating, thundering over hills ten thousand strong, and gathering, mousey-still, around a little hole in the ground to see a man push a little ball into the bottom of it with a crooked iron stick. (Paul Gallico)

33c (1) Exercise 10

Streamline the following passages by changing empty verbs and unnecessary nominalizations to strong verbs.

1. In this morning's meeting, the club president made note of the number of people who were participants in the recreation program. She also made comments on the club's desire to offer support for the program next year. The treasurer then made the suggestion that we conduct a survey of members to find out how many have intentions of becoming participants next year.

2. Scientists hold the belief that the common cold is not a single disease. They have made the discovery that about 200 different viruses are the causes of infections. The experts, however, do not possess much knowledge about how colds are transmitted. Some have made the conclusion that the viruses can be transmitted through the air. Others believe that colds are the result of direct contact. In any case, since people cannot maintain isolation from others, they cannot find an escape from colds.

33c (2) Exercise 11

Change the following passive-voice sentences to active. When no *by* or *with* phrase exists, you will have to supply an appropriate active-voice subject.

EXAMPLE: Piles of spicy crabs and boiled corn were eaten. → We ate piles of spicy crabs and boiled corn.

1. Hypnosis has been used by psychologists for more than a century.
2. The mountains were covered with snow.
3. Almost any plant can be composted for use in the garden.

4. Cheese was used as a food source more than 4,000 years ago.
5. *Mean Streets* was filmed by Martin Scorsese in New York City's Little Italy.
6. The language in policies is being simplified by insurance companies.
7. Our lifestyles would be changed drastically by energy shortages.
8. The journal is published by a local press.
9. My bank was robbed this morning.
10. A touchdown was made in the last three seconds of the game.

33c (3) Exercise 12

Streamline the following passage by eliminating any unnecessary *that, who* and *which* clauses.

During the depression, a newspaper editor, who was from Oklahoma City, toured twenty states. In Washington, he reported his findings to a committee that was conducting hearings on unemployment. He told of conditions that were deplorable in the states that he had visited. He saw counties, which were once prosperous coal-mining regions, without a single bank. In Seattle, he saw women who were searching for scraps of food in refuse piles. He read of sheep raisers who were desperate and who were killing their sheep because they could get only a dollar a head. In the South, he saw bales of cotton that were rotting in the fields. He sympathized with all these people who were victims of circumstances that were uncontrollable, and he warned the committee of conditions that were worsening.

33c (4) Exercise 13

Streamline the following sentence by splitting it into more than one sentence and getting rid of any unnecessary words.

When Jones made the final shot that put the Knicks out in front just before the buzzer sounded to end the game, the excited fans were cheering and stomping so loudly that they did not realize that the official had blown the whistle to serve as a signal that someone had committed a foul and that the basket might possibly not count and the game could be lost.

33c (5) Exercise 14

Streamline the following passage by making clear the connection between subjects and verbs.

The first American mule, bred two hundred years ago by George Washington from a Virginia mare and a Spanish jack named Royal Gift, a present from the King of Spain, began a revolution in draft animals. The mule, which is hardier than a horse, more resistant to disease, better able to tolerate intense heat, more sure-footed, and more intelligent, was invaluable before the Industrial Revolution. Mules cultivated cotton on southern plantations, toiled in coal mines, and transported goods across the desert. And of course, mules, which could carry weapons and supplies in terrain where trucks and jeeps were helpless to move, served in both world wars.

33c Exercise 15

Using the techniques discussed in 33c, streamline the following passage.

The idea that Shakespeare's plays were written not by William Shakespeare himself but by some strange and shy genius hiding behind a pen name is one of the silliest literary theories ever to be proposed. "Real authors," from Ben Johnson and Christopher Marlowe to Queen Elizabeth and the Rosicrucians, are constantly being proposed by critics and amateur sleuths who believe that William Shakespeare was a simple-minded hick, who was possibly illiterate and did not have the background to make references to law, navigation, medicine, history, and court life, and that the records of Shakespeare's life are too scarce for someone who was so popular in his lifetime.

In fact, both of these ideas are invalid. First, Shakespeare's plays do not contain any information that would have been unavailable to any Elizabethan with a few books, and furthermore, the references made to geography and history are often mixed up and inaccurate; second, we know as much about Shakespeare's life as we know about the lives of many other famous Elizabethan authors whose work is not questioned.

The idea that some famous person would probably not have picked the name of an illiterate nobody to use as a pen name never seems to be considered by the "Shakespeare hunters."

33d Exercise 16

Identify the kinds of figurative language used in the following quotations.

1. "The face of the sea is always changing.... Its aspects and moods vary hour by hour." (Rachel Carson, *The Sea Around Us*)

2. "Although one may fail to find happiness in theatrical life, one never wishes to give it up after having once tasted its fruits. To enter the School of the Imperial Ballet is to enter a convent whence frivolity is banned, and where merciless discipline reigns. (Anna Pavlova, "Pages of My Life," *Pavlova: A Biography*)

3. "The solar system as a whole, like a merry-go-round unhinged, spins, bobs, and blinks at the speed of 43,200 miles an hour along a course set east of Hercules." (Annie Dillard, *Pilgrim at Tinker Creek*)

4. "For a brief moment of time [clipper ships] flashed their splendor around the world, then disappeared with the sudden completeness of a wild pigeon." (Samuel Eliot Morison, *Maritime History of Massachusetts*)

5. "The fox was desperately close. Auntie Mame switched on the ignition and the car bounded forward just as a small cannon ball of black fur darted into the road. There was a terrible screech of brakes and I was thrown forward against the windshield. Then all hell broke loose. Hounds, horses, and riders descended on us like an avalanche. Nearly three dozen riders were thrown, and two big bay mares rammed into the Dusenberg so hard the front fender and hood had to be replaced. A third mount was half in and half out of the back seat, whinnying horribly. All in all, there were more horses shot that day than at the Battle of Gettysburg." (Patrick Dennis, *Auntie Mame*)

33d Exercise 17

Use your imagination to change the literal language of these statements to figurative language.

EXAMPLE: The sentence was long and confusing. → The sentence encircled and choked the meaning like a giant boa constrictor.

1. His opponent in the tennis match was fearsome.
2. The book was boring.
3. The plane ride was extremely rough.
4. Hate made him irrational.
5. The hurricane destroyed the town.

33e   Exercise 18

1. Rewrite these two sentences to make the sound echo the sense. Remember that unstressed syllables speed up the pace and stressed syllables slow it down.

   The small boy ran down the road so fast that the dust rose behind him like the wake created by a power boat.

   The moon came slowly up over the leafy trees, throwing a kind of eerie light over the garden where we sitting.

2. Try using sounds and rhythms in the following passage to suggest the light, airy quality of the comforter.

   The comforter that my grandmother gave me when I was fifteen was very large, but it weighed hardly anything. I would sleep under it and stay very warm, but I didn't feel like any weight was on my body.

3. Rewrite the following passage so that the rhythm suggests what the rider and horse are doing. The beginning of the passage should suggest a relaxed pace. Then the rhythm should get faster as the horse begins to run. Finally, the last sentence should reverse the pace and end with the word *Snip*.

   I spent my youth on a horse. His name was Snip. He was half quarter horse and half palomino. Whenever I was not in school, we would go off and spend the day in the hills and creeks. He would seem content enough while we were out, but at the end of the ride, when he could see the barn door, he would start to run. No pulling back on the reins could stop him. His shoulders would heave. His massive head would bob. He would breathe heavily. He would frantically try to lessen the distance between himself and the barn. He would go faster and faster headed home. I feel like Snip sometimes these days.

4. The rhythm of the following passage is choppy and abrupt. Try rewriting to suggest a floating could of pollen that spreads ominously like something in a horror movie.

For many people, robins and jonquils are the first indications of spring. But for allergy sufferers, spring begins with an ominous cloud of yellow pollen. This pollen floats through the air. It is inside and outside. It covers cars. The pollen also gets on sidewalks and bushes. In the house it settles on bric-a-brac. As a matter of fact, it covers everything that doesn't move fast.

PART IV: REVIEW EXERCISES

1. Improve the word choice in the following passages.

a. The physical requirements of a television news anchor are very rigid. First, he must be old enough to seem mature and young enough to seem with it. Second, he must have a face that will appeal to the man in the street, not too serious or grim but not too laid back. Third, he must be perfectly groomed, with every hair in place. Fourth, he can be neither skinny nor corpulent. In other words, his looks must appeal to every possible viewer—the corporate businessman, the housewife, the postman, the coed.

b. We have an uphill battle making asbestos contamination control efforts in virtually all sectors of the environment. Our tried and true methods of cleaning up have not always made the grade. Now we need to combine together to prioritize solutions. In the interest of the environment, we must eliminate the helter-skelter removal of asbestos materials. The public is aware of the problem and demands action but opposes any revenue enhancement at this point in time. Minimizing wastes and utilizing asbestos contamination abatement procedures are easier said than done. The safest techniques, needless to say, are also the most financially demanding, but it is better late than never.

c. In this day and age, the number of senior citizens has proliferated by leaps and bounds. The average life span was in the vicinity of fifty in 1910, but subsequent to improved quality of life, the old-timers can anticipate kicking up their heels till age seventy-five. Because of pensions and Social Security benefits, a number of these senior citizens will find rest and relaxation at a ripe old age in comfortable retirement villages. Lucky retirees, young in spirit, could spend their golden years in localities such as Saint Petersburg, Florida.

2. Improve the structures in the following passages by combining, separating, or rearranging structures; by streamlining to remove weak and wordy prose; and by changing the sound and rhythm.

a. In 1906, Upon Sinclair wrote *The Jungle*. He was only 28. The novel exposed the filthy conditions in Chicago's meat-packing industry. It was based on facts that were published in a 1904 study. The novel caused a furor. In the book, the main character is Jurgis Rudkus, a Slav immigrant. He goes to work in the Chicago stockyards. While he is there, he suffers the filth, disease, brutality, and helplessness of a typical packing worker. He and his wife, whose name is Ona, because of filthy working and living conditions, are attacked by disease; they are forced by their poverty to endure cold winters and flies in the summers. Eventually Ona dies in childbirth; previously, they had eaten bad food or, when Rudkus was laid off, no food. Because of the horrible working conditions that were exposed by the novel, reform was called for by many groups. The American Medical Association sought reform in the food industry. Theodore Roosevelt, as result of the novel, began an investigation. As a result of the investigation, the Pure Food and Drugs Act was passed.

b. Two current issues that have led to an increased interest in mathematics are the feminist movement with its concern about women being excluded from any scientific or technical careers and educational reform with the general concern about students not getting the basic skills necessary to pursue advanced education. A person's attitude toward mathematics is what underlies both these issues. If a student has the expectation that mathematics challenges a person's highest creative abilities, helps a person to think clearly, provides good mental exercise, then this student's attitude will be an attitude that will probably lead to success. A student who has the belief that mathematics is busy work, that it is too hard, that it is too abstract will more than likely be a student who will not succeed in mathematics courses. Good mathematics students usually have the understanding that mathematics has been important to the advance of civilization; poor mathematics students do not have any realization of mathematics' value to society. The attitudes of these poor students are going to limit their opportunities for careers and make them anxious about mathematics for the rest of their lives. Not only should mathematical skills be taught by school teachers and other educators, but also attitudes toward mathematics should be emphasized.

c. In 1868, an act was passed by Congress that set forth the use of stamp taxes on liquor. The number of tax agents were increased, and the conflict between the moonshiners and the revenuers was started. Between 1880 and 1895, the number of seizures of moonshining stills was doubled. The confrontations, which sometimes reached the size of full-scale battles, caused carbines to be issued to the tax collectors and posses to be authorized. One of the severest battles that was ever fought between government agents and moonshiners occurred in 1878 in Overton County, Tennessee, where 10 government men were beseiged in a farmhouse by 25 moonshiners who were led by the notorious Campbell Morgan. Finally, a negotiated settlement that was reached made the specification that everyone would stop shooting and that Morgan would turn himself in—but not to the leader of the government men. A story that was developed about this time has a young revenuer who makes the discovery of a mountain shack ask a young boy about the whereabouts of his father. The boy replies that his father is away making moonshine. The agent, who offers to give the boy fifty cents to take him to the site, tells the boy, who holds out his hand, that the money will be given on their return. "I will take the money now," is what the boy says, "for you ain't coming back."

PART V

The Writing Process

Chapter 34

THE SEARCH FOR IDEAS

34a Exercise 1

Keep a journal and write in it freely and frequently, even including material that at the time seems to lead nowhere. You never know what will be productive later on. The more you write, the more likely you are to find a good subject or to accumulate supporting details. Here are some suggestions about the sort of material you might include.

remembrances of early years
impressions of books or films
details about parties or vacations
descriptions of people at a concert, play, or athletic event
reactions to personal stories from a local newspaper
sketches of your family or friends
plans for the future
summaries of class discussions or conversations
opinions about current issues
ideas for improvements

34b Exercise 2

Try meditation to find a subject for writing. If nothing comes immediately to mind, you might start by thinking about one of the subjects listed here. But do not try to stick to a topic. Just let your mind range wherever it will.

solutions to problems
moving to another place

past mistakes
the dangers of drugs
the worst jobs
the changing planet
future transportation
life without education
breaking up
breaking away

34c Exercise 3

For ten minutes, brainstorm a topic by writing down anything that comes to mind. Begin with a topic such as one in the following list.

a favorite car
reasons that students drop out of college
problems in your community
the relationship between people and pets
a good job
the effect of abolishing grades
peer pressure on teenagers
gaining independence

After the ten minutes, read over your notes. Pick an idea or potential idea and repeat the process for another ten minutes to find at least one idea that might be developed into a complete paper. If you still have no idea for a paper, go through the process again or start over with another potential topic.

34d Exercise 4

Write the word *entertainment* in the center of a sheet of paper, circle it, and then use the clustering technique for ten minutes. Find a cluster that looks interesting, and write that cluster on a fresh sheet of paper. Repeat the clustering technique for another ten minutes. Then look over the pages for an idea that could be developed into a paper. If you find no idea, try the technique with other nucleus words such as *weather, noise, school, telephone, family, travel, cheating,* and *food.*

34e   Exercise 5

For about fifteen minutes, write your thoughts as fast as you can, trying not to be critical or analytical. When you have lapses, scribble or write nonsense, but do not stop the momentum of putting something down on paper. To get started, you might pick an issue, such as one of the following.

smoking in public places
TV violence
crime prevention
consumer safety
prejudice
pollution
exercise and health
weaknesses in American schools
health services for students
traffic and parking problems
student employment

When time is up, read what you have written. and list any ideas that might serve as a subject or be useful in paper.

34f Exercise 6

For five of the following subjects, create ladders with four rungs, moving from the general or abstract to the specific or concrete.

humor	jealousy	games	conflict
contests	school	food	careers
television	celebrations	cars	hunting

34g Exercise 7

Use questions to explore one topic in each category. Write four to six questions for each of the subjects you choose. From your questions, pick two that might be developed into a paper. (Remember that not all of the questions will be appropriate for every subject and that other questions can be added as they come to mind.)

1. *object or device:* a painting, stereo, sculpture, motorcycle, lawn mower, typewriter, map, doll, toy, computer
2. *process:* painting a house, riding a skateboard, flying a kite, playing a particular card game, interviewing for a job, studying for a test, exercising
3. *person:* coach, preacher, teacher, relative, doctor, dentist, friend
4. *place:* your neighborhood, city, town, or state; a place of employment; your old grammar school; a video game arcade; a bowling alley; a golf course; a museum; a summer camp
5. *event:* rock concert, sporting event, trial, accident, college registration, initiation into a club, wedding, high school graduation trip
6. *idea or abstraction:* pride, greed, ambition, confusion, misunderstanding, fear, frustration, peace of mind
7. *problem:* employment, housing, marriage, money, parents, transportation, crime, violence, overpopulation
8. *judgment or opinion:* The minimum wage law should/should not apply to those under twenty years of age. College athletes should/should not be required to take courses the semesters they compete. The quality of American cars is/is not equal to that of Japanese cars. Campus parking places should/should not be determined by lottery.

34h Exercise 8

Use the classical topics to generate ideas about one of the following subjects. If none of the subjects appeals to you, use another. List at least one narrowed subject for each topic: definition, comparison, relationship, circumstance, and testimony.

the architecture in a particular region
space colonization
rock and roll
illiteracy
holiday depression
romance novels
fear of flying
racquetball
pornography
beauty pageants

34i Exercise 9

Find three potential subjects by reading, listening to radio, watching television, or talking to people. If a subject is too general or too abstract, you can use another technique such as brainstorming or asking logical questions to make the subject suitable.

Chapter 35

DECISIONS

35a Exercise 1

Usually, you can adapt a topic to any purpose. For example, you could write on the topic *SAT tests* with all four purposes.

Impression	My fear when I took the SAT test
Information	Effective ways to study for the SAT test
Argument	The SAT test is unfair to disadvantaged students.
Entertainment	Amusing strategies students use to prepare for the SAT test

Try to adapt the following topics to two or more of the four purposes.

1. gang activities
2. computers
3. childhood games
4. classroom discipline
5. overpopulation
6. boxing
7. maps
8. horror movies
9. fast food
10. cowboy boots

35b Exercise 2

The following statements are all on the same subject—steroids. Their intended audiences, however, are different. What differences can you detect?

1. "Throughout history athletes have looked for that extra edge that would assure them a superior performance in competition. For over three decades some have claimed to have found that edge through hormonal manipulation with chemical substances known as steroids."

2. "Experimental studies in both animals and humans have showed that steroids possess both anabolic and androgenic actions. The androgenic actions of steroids are those actions involving the development and maintenance of primary and secondary sexual characteristics, while the anabolic actions consist of the positive effects of promoting protein synthesis and muscle growth."

3. "I was in bad shape, very bad shape. From the steroids. It had all come down from the steroids, the crap I'd taken to get big and strong and aggressive so I could play the game I love."

35b   Exercise 3

The following three passages are by the same author, John C. Lilly, and on the same subject, dolphins. What audience do you think Lilly was addressing in each?

1. "Eventually it may be possible for humans to speak with another species. I have come to this conclusion after careful consideration of evidence gained through my research experiments with dolphins."

2. "For picking up and transmitting the airborne voice output of the dolphin and the speech output of the human, either two Shure model 545 Unidyne II microphones were used or a model 545 plus a Lavalier model 560."

3. "Some of the sonic (audible to human beings) emissions of the bottle-nose dolphin of the east coast of the United States (*Tursiops truncatus* Montagu) have been described."

35a–35c   Exercise 4

For each passage, try to identify the writer's purpose (impression, information, argument, or entertainment). Then determine whether the passage is written for a general or a specific audience. Finally, describe the voice of each passage. Is it detached or involved? Solemn or humorous? Liberal or conservative? Formal or informal?

1. The Pleistocene American mastodon, *Mammut americanum* . . . was quite large, reaching the size of our present day Indian elephant, perhaps even larger. The word *Mammut* means "earth borrower," and it can be traced back to the Middle Ages, when eastern European farmers found gigantic bones in their fields and believed that they belonged to some monstrous burrowing beast. (S. C. Knox and Sue Pitts)

2. Birth rates indicate that the number of high school graduates is decreasing and will not increase until 1998. Sociological studies show approximately 40 million adults in transition; these transitions include career change, unemployment, divorce, and widowhood. Furthermore, the median age in the U.S. is now 31. These demographic facts demonstrate clearly that the adult-student market in higher education is increasing. Thus, while you must continue to recruit students from the traditional-aged market, it is a serious mistake for you to concentrate all your efforts on that market. (B. Carter and C. Tullos)

3. Should your political opinions be at extreme variance with those of your parents, keep in mind that while it is indeed your constitutional right to express these sentiments verbally, it is unseemly to do so with your mouth full—particularly when it is full of the oppressor's standing rib roast. (Fran Lebowitz)

4. We found the cave up a side canyon, the entrance blocked with fallen boulders. Even to my youthful eyes it looked old, incredibly old. The waters and the frosts for centuries had eaten at the boulders and gnawed the cave. Down by the vanished stream bed a little gleam of worked flints caught our eye. (Loren Eiseley)

5. We are satisfied with justice, if the court knows what justice is, or if any human being can tell what justice is. If anybody can look into the minds and hearts and the lives and the origin of these two youths and tell what justice is, we would be content. But nobody can do it without imagination, without sympathy, without kindliness, without understanding, and I have faith that this Court will take this case, with his conscience, and his judgment and his courage and save these boys' lives. (Clarence Darrow)

35a–35c Exercise 5

Imagine a logical purpose, audience, and voice for the following subjects.

1. how to study for a history test
2. an improvement needed in your community
3. a holiday that should be added to your school's calendar
4. the safety of generic drugs
5. steps for avoiding a mugging
6. an evaluation of a textbook
7. an overrated entertainer
8. the car you would drive if money were no object
9. the season of the year you enjoy most
10. a subject that you find through such techniques as keeping a journal, brainstorming, or research

35d Exercise 6

Which of the following do not meet the requirements for a suitable thesis? For each unacceptable thesis, state which requirements are lacking.

1. Telecommunications is an interesting field of study.
2. Although Frank Lloyd Wright made his reputation as an innovator, he was actually an imitator.
3. The four types of stress are mental, physical, chemical, and thermal.
4. A rumor circulated in 1978 that a fast-food chain put earthworms in hamburger meat to increase the protein content.
5. All nature is not beautiful.
6. Astrological profiles are silly.
7. Advice from a freshman in college to a high school student.
8. More marriages would survive if people signed premarital contracts.
9. Although many viewers love Mayberry in the *Andy Griffith Show,* few of them would like to live there.
10. Rock stars go to extremes to be different.

35d   Exercise 7

Write a thesis for five of the following subjects. Instead of simply turning each phrase into a sentence, narrow the subject by making a specific statement.

EXAMPLE: Cooking as a hobby → Learning to cook is an effective
                 way to improve your social life.

in search of a decent hamburger
Tarzan as a romantic hero
how computers are changing society
status symbols in the middle class
the ultimate stereo equipment
the hardships of a tourist
part-time jobs for the untrained
magazines and their intended audiences
advice about studying
economizing in college
unsympathetic teachers
living alone
romance through personal advertisements
self-defense for women
telephone options

35e   Exercise 8

What pattern or patterns are suggested by each of the following controlling ideas?

1.   Four strategies will help you remember names and faces.
2.   The Hubble Space Telescope has made astronomers revise their image of the universe.
3.   Some theorists believe that most human behavior is learned, whereas others believe that humans are biologically programmed for particular behavioral patterns.
4.   During his boxing career, Muhammad Ali's charisma was as remarkable as his physical prowess.
5.   Over one hundred years of struggle preceded the opening of the Panama Canal in 1920.
6.   The establishment of a food plaza would help attract shoppers to the depressed downtown area.

7. The compulsive consumer is a recognizable species.
8. This year's coverage of the Super Bowl typified excessive network hype.
9. Hollywood's biblical epics are more fantastic than religious.
10. Painting with watercolors is a better hobby than painting with oils.
11. Gardening programs in housing projects discourage vandalism.
12. Blue jeans can be classified by their purpose: to be practical or to be fashionable.
13. In exercise classes, differences between personality types are exaggerated.
14. There are three components of an effective letter of application.
15. Everyone needs to take a few business courses.

35f Exercise 9

Outlines can reveal problems with the subject of a proposed paper, the content, and the organization. What problems do the following outlines reveal?

There are obstacles to the widespread use of the bicycle as transportation in the U.S.

Distances
Automobile and truck traffic
Bicycle use in Europe
Thievery

Since their introduction, Christmas cards have changed.

1. Now cards are often humorous.
2. Cards reflect sophisticated production techniques.

Unlike previous painters, impressionistic painters painted everyday pastimes.

1. Edouard Manet's *Boating*
2. August Renoir's *Rower's Lunch*
3. Claude Monet's interest in light and color
4. Edgar Degas' *Carriage at the Races*
5. Earlier artists' emphasis on noble and classical subjects

Advertising about weight reduction is often deceptive.
—Promise of immediate results
—Promise of sexual attractiveness
—Implication of effortlessness
—Misleading testimonials
—Medical jargon
—Exercising unnecessary
—Magical foods or pills

Some inventions have changed civilization.
  I. Early Inventions
      A.   Bow and Arrow
      B.   Drill
      C.   Plow
 II. The Printing Press
III. The Industrial Revolution
      A.   Steam Engine
      B.   Power Loom
 IV. Leonardo da Vinci's Inventions
  V. Gunpowder
 VI. Recent Inventions

35f Exercise 10

Write working outlines to develop three of the following ideas.

1. The Japanese education system is more rigorous than the American system.
2. People can be classified by the kinds of vacations they take.
3. Seeing a movie in a theater is a different experience from seeing one on television.
4. Christmas is typically a time of stress.
5. Some college classes make me wonder what I'm paying for.
6. The problem with television is that it makes us too passive.
7. Magazine racks in stores tell us something about interests of Americans.
8. Women's clothes are designed for ultrathin models, not for normal figures.
9. Consequences for misbehavior change as one grows older.
10. Elaborate weddings are a waste of money.

Chapter 36

PARAGRAPHS

36a (1) Exercise 1

Identify the topic sentences of the following passages. If no topic sentence is present, state it in your own words.

1. In high school classes, students are expected to follow instructions unquestioningly. The main emphasis is on behavior and order. On tests students are required to repeat information or to check true–false answers. Curiosity and originality are discouraged. In fact, America's schools are breeding conformity.

2. When I visit a museum containing antique clothing, I am amazed at the difficulties people in the past must have had dressing. Everything was fastened by ties or buttons, no snaps and no zippers. All the clothes look very uncomfortable—constrictive, stiff, and layered. The shoes for the right and left feet were identical. I'm told that it wasn't until the mid-nineteenth century that shoes were designed to fit the different shapes of both feet.

3. Adults returning to school must sacrifice time with their families and sometimes sacrifice their accustomed standards of living. They often suffer doubts about their skills because of long periods of scholastic inactivity. Also, they may feel out of place surrounded by the younger students.

4. My childhood friends were called Boopie, Boo, Puddin, Cooter, and Bobo. At age twenty, these people are still known as Boopie, Boo, Puddin, Cooter, and Bobo. If anyone called them Susan, Marshall, Helen, Edward, or Chester, they probably wouldn't know immediately who was being addressed. Nicknames are hard to get

rid of, especially in a small town. You might be able to move away and use the name on your birth certificate, but at home you will always have to answer to a nickname.

5. Customers who order pizza to be delivered to their homes or dormitory rooms have peculiar senses of humor. Some call in orders for places and rooms that don't exist. Others give addresses of people who have not ordered pizzas. Once, three drivers from three pizza restaurants showed up at the same time at the same house, and no one who lived there and placed the order.

Some customers also find it hilarious to order strange combinations like triple anchovy, triple shrimp, and triple jalapeño peppers. Others order weird proportions like one-third ham and sausage, one-third ham and hamburger, and one-third hamburger and sausage, mushrooms on the third with ham and sausage, peppers on the third with ham and hamburger, olives and onions on the third with hamburger and sausage, and hold the cheese.

36a (2) Exercise 2

Identify the organizational patterns used in each of the following paragraphs.

1. I keep emphasizing how dramatically things have changed; this is necessary because the scale of change is so enormous that it is far too easy to under estimate it. A useful analogy can be made with motor cars to put things in perspective. Today's car differs from those of the immediate post-war years on a number of counts. It is cheaper, allowing for the ravages of inflation, and it is more economical and efficient. All this can be put down to advances in automobile engineering, more efficient methods of production, and a wider market. But suppose for a moment that the automobile industry had developed at the same rate as computers and over the same period: how much cheaper and more efficient would the current models be? If you have not already heard the analogy the answer is shattering. Today you would be able to buy a Rolls-Royce for $2.75, it would do three million miles to the gallon, and it would deliver enough power to drive the *Queen Elizabeth II.* And if you were interested in miniaturization, you could place half a dozen of them on a pinhead. (Christopher Evans, *The Micro Millennium*)

2. The expansion of English around the world has been matched by the infiltration of English words into the vocabularies of dozens of other countries. Japanese sports fans talk knowledgeably of *beisuboru* and *garafu* (golf) over glasses of *koka-kora;* Spanish speakers, sometimes stimulated by too many *cocteles,* wax frenetic over *futbol,* while their newspaper *columnistas* deplore the spread of *gangsterismo.* West German newspapers run *Reporten* of legislative *Hearings* on *das Fallout* and *die Recession,* and cover *Press Konferenzen* complete with *no Komment* and *off die Rekord;* in France, *teenagers* (pronounced "teenahz*hair*") wearing blue *djins* buy *hot dogues* from street vendors. (Robert Claiborne, *Our Marvelous Native Tongue*)

3. Did you even wonder why Mr. Rogers can do a children's television show day after day with the same kind, loving, gentle, understanding, and perfectly rational demeanor? Has it ever struck you as slightly odd that he can relate warmly and patiently to children with nary a whine or a whimper to say nothing of a scream? One day recently I finally discovered it's because he rarely has a child on his show. All his children are located conveniently thousands of miles away from him on the other side of the television screen. (Will Manley, "Facing the Public," *Wilson Library Bulletin*)

4. In academe, the number of courses on medieval subjects has been on the rise for several years, as has the number of students taking them. According to a survey by the medievalists Christopher Kleinhenz and Frank Gentry, during the decade ending in 1980 thirty-seven new scholarly journals specializing in the Middle Ages commenced publication. Since 1970, attendance at the annual conference of the Medieval Institute, at Western Michigan University, in Kalamazoo, has swelled from 800 to almost 2,000, making it the largest medieval *congressus* in the world. (Cullen Murphy, "Nostalgia for the Dark Ages," *Atlantic*)

5. The printed page was itself a highly specialized (and spatialized) term of communication. In 1500 A.D. it was revolutionary. And Erasmus was perhaps the first to grasp the fact that the revolution was going to occur above all in the classroom. He devoted himself to the production of textbooks and to the setting up of grammar schools. The printed book soon liquidated two thousand years of manuscript culture. It created the solitary student. It set up the rule of private interpretation against public disputation. It

established the divorce between "literature and life." It created a new and highly abstract culture because it was itself a mechanized form of culture. Today, when the textbook has yielded to the classroom project and the classroom as social workshop and discussion group, it is easier for us to notice what was going on in 1500. Today we know that the turn to the visual on one hand, that is, to photography, and to the auditory media of radio and public address systems on the other hand, has created a totally new environment for the educational process. (Marshall McLuhan, "Sight, Sound, and the Fury," *Commonweal*)

6. Although I didn't realize it at the time, scientists generally divide into two camps, abstractionists and experimentalists. The theorists and the tinkerers. Especially in the physical sciences, the distinction can be spotted straight off. It has since been my observation that, in addition to their skills in the lab, the latter group (particularly the males) can fix things around the house, know what's happening under the hood of a car, and have a special appeal to the opposite sex. Theorists stick to their own gifts, like engaging themselves for hours with a mostly blank sheet of paper and discussing chess problems at lunch. Sometime in college, either by genes or accident, a budding scientist starts drifting one way or the other. From then on, things are pretty much settled. (Alan Lightman, "A Flash of Light," *Science 84*)

36a (3) Exercise 3

Suggest strategies that you could use to develop the following subjects into paragraphs or blocks.

1. the expense of owning a dog
2. the monotony of American motels
3. American beer versus imported beer
4. types of parents
5. the consequences of sleeping late
6. T-shirt messages
7. the problems of working students
8. a tour of your hometown
9. effective excuses
10. the appeal of professional wrestling

36a (3) Exercise 4

Choose three topics (topics of your own or from Exercise 3), and develop each in a paragraph or block of paragraphs using one of the suggested strategies or a combination of strategies.

36b Exercise 5

In each of these introductions, identify the technique or techniques used.

1. Introduction to an essay on the frequency of new discoveries in anthropology

   My first teacher of paleontology was almost as old as some of the animals he discussed. He lectured from notes on yellow foolscap that he must have assembled during his own days in graduate school. The words changed not at all from year to year, but the paper got older and older. I sat in the first row, bathed in yellow dust, as the paper cracked and crumbled every time he turned the page.

   It is a blessing that he never had to lecture on human evolution. New and significant prehuman fossils have been unearthed with such unrelenting frequency in recent years that the fate of any lecture notes can only be described with the watchword of a fundamentally irrational economy—planned obsolescence. Each year, when the topic comes up in my courses, I simply open my old folder and dump the contents into the nearest circular file. And here we go again. (Stephen Jay Gould, "Bushes and Ladders in Human Evolution," *Ever Since Darwin*)

2. Introduction to a report on theories about bird migration

   The melancholy appearance of geese passing south under low autumn skies is as much a mark of the turning seasons as the first robin of spring. Some of us pay more attention to these things than others, but few are more drawn to the seasonal movement of birds than ornithologists who have for years been attempting to understand one of migration's most vexing riddles: How do birds know which way to go? (Patrick Cook, "How Do Birds Find Where They're Going?" *Science 84*)

3. Introduction to an essay on American wastefulness

    Cans. Beer cans. Glinting on the verges of a million miles of
    roadways, lying in scrub, grass, dirt, leaves, sand, mud, but never
    hidden. Piels, Rheingold, Ballantine, Schaefer, Schlitz, shining in
    the sun or picked by moon or the beams of headlights at night;
    washed by rain or flattened by wheels, but never dulled, never
    buried, never destroyed. Here is the mark of savages, the
    testament of wasters, the stain of prosperity. (Marya Mannes,
    "Wasteland," *More in Anger*)

4. Introduction to an article on a new fishing boat

    It never fails. As soon as times get better, everyone starts
    introducing newer, bigger boats. In one sense that's good for you,
    the boatman, for it allows you a more diverse arena in which to
    make your selection.

    But unfortunately, another side darkens this new prosperity.
    Occasionally, such new boats are born of a haste to fill a perceived
    void in the manufacturer's line, and the final product shows it.
    Even worse, we see special-purpose boats—sportfishermen, for
    example—being introduced by companies lacking the experience
    or expertise to build them. (Richard Thiel, "Tiara 3600 Pursuit,"
    Boating)

5. Introduction to a humorous essay on the struggle between people
    and things

    Inanimate objects are classified into three major categories—
    those that don't work, those that break down and those that get
    lost. (Russell Baker, "The Plot Against People," *New York Times*)

6. Introduction to a report on the dialects of bees

    For almost two decades my colleagues and I have been studying
    one of the most remarkable systems of communication that
    nature has evolved. This is the "language" of the bees: the dancing
    movements by which forager bees direct their hivemates, with
    great precision, to a source of food. In our earliest work we had
    to look for the means by which the insects communicate and,
    once we found it, to learn to read the language.

    Then we discovered that different varieties of the honeybee
    use the same basic patterns in slightly different ways; that they
    speak different dialects, as it were. This led us to examine the

dances of other species in the hope of discovering the evolution of this marvelously complex behavior. Our investigation has thus taken us into the field of comparative linguistics. (Karl von Frisch, "Dialects in the Language of Bees," *Scientific American*)

36b Exercise 6

Write introductions suitable for papers on two of the following subjects. If none of the subjects seems appealing, supply two of your own.

a proposal for changes in NFL rules
a formula for writing horoscopes and never being wrong
folk remedies that work
the etiquette of coed dormitories
a classification of recreational vehicles by types of owners
effective ways to fight depression
types of television game shows
body building: for men only?
ridiculous Christmas presents
the expense of entertainment
strange pets
shopping by mail-oder catalog

36c Exercise 7

What typical concluding strategies or combination of strategies do you find in the following passages?

1. Technology and discoveries have radically changed dentistry. Children no longer have cavities as they once did, and adults no longer lose their teeth. Also, the equipment dentists use is costing more and more. Thus, students looking for a profitable profession should look toward other fields, not toward dentistry.

2. Over the years, a London art dealer collected the 425 photographs contained in this interesting but expensive album. Pictured are not only famous artists such as Whistler, Sargent, and Degas but also their friends and followers. The vivid likenesses bring the Victorian era to life; *The Victorian Art World* is well worth its price.

3. But before tanning salons can be considered safe, studies must be done on the long-range effects of ultraviolet A-rays on the human body.

4. In summary, many experts recognize six types of intelligence: linguistic, musical, spatial, logical/mathematical, kinesthetic, and personal. And as the case studies above demonstrate, parents should encourage their children's strengths and not worry unduly about weaknesses. As Dr. Wilkerson puts it, "People aren't happy doing things they don't do well."

5. So if your medical problem is not an emergency, compare several doctors. Ask where they went to medical school Find out if they have up-to-date equipment. Check to see if their office personnel are pleasant and efficient. Investigate their fees. Surely you should spend as much time shopping for health care as you do for a car.

36c Exercise 8

Write a suitable conclusion for two of the following papers.

1. A paper that evaluates a current movie
2. A paper that develops the following controlling idea: Attitude affects one's success in school.
3. A paper that attempts to solve the problem of massive unemployment among young people
4. A paper on dictionaries and books of synonyms; the paper begins with Mark Twain's statement, "The difference between the almost right word and the right word is the difference between the lightning bug and the lightning."
5. A paper that contains evidence that acid rain is damaging our land and water life, eroding our structures, and even threatening our health

Chapter 37

REVISION

37a–37e Exercise 1

Two rough drafts of student papers follow. Revise each, using these questions as guides.

(1) Is the thesis clear?
(2) Does everything in the paper relate to the thesis?
(3) Is the organization clear?
(4) Is there adequate connection between sentences and paragraphs?
(5) Are there stylistic weaknesses?
(6) Are there errors in grammar, punctuation, and mechanics?
(7) Are there any spelling errors?

A.

Many people view retarded children as freaks. Some ignore these children. Some are even afraid of them. I must admit to having these feelings about retarded children when I first worked with them.

When I first worked with retarded children, I was nervous to say the least. I do not know what I expected the children to be like. I was not prepared for my first meeting with them. The children seemed shockingly pitiful. Some looked as if they were not even aware of their own existance. One child aimlessly walked in circles, another stood swaying from side to side. Children wildly ran around in another room and shouted at each other.

As an assignment for a child psychology class I had to spend twenty hours observing children. I decided to spend my time observing retarded children. I wanted to find out what they were really like. I wanted to know why I was afraid of retarded children.

The school for retarded children is well staffed. The teachers read to the children. They taught practical things like the meaning of traffic lights, the names of coins and bills in our currency system, and table manners.

As the days went by, I got aquainted with the children. They were not always easy to manage, but "normal" children are not easy to manage either. On one occasion I accompanied the class on a field trip to a fire station and to McDonald's. I was very apprehencive about going to eat at McDonald's. I kept wondering how the children were going to act in public. I was sure I would be embarrassed in one way or another but I was wrong. The children ate hamburgers and played on the playground as any other children would have done. They did not go wild as I had expected, they just had a good time. This surprised me.

I realized that those children, although handicapped, are not very different from other children. Sometimes a retarded child is good. Other times they are bad. They were no longer the wild demons of my first impression, they were just children.

B.

You might want to get rid of a roomate for a variety of reasons. You realy hate the person or you have a friend who needs a place to live and wants to move into your apartment with you or your roomate is a very nice person but never has any money and so cannot pay his share of the expenses. A good roomate is compatible with you, is always considerate, and is willing to compromise.

Their are a number of tactics you can use to get rid of an unwanted roomate. You need a carefully planned scheme that begins with little things and work up to more drastic measures. This keeps you from being any nastier than necessary. If the little measures work your roomate might leave while you can still to friends. If you are friends. Also the real nasty measures could lead to retaliation by physical violance or legal action. In stage one you can do little things such as leaving dirty dishes in the sink, filling up the refrigerator with speciments from your biology lab, taking long showers that use up all the hot water. You can also wet his toothbrush so that he will suspect you have been using it. And you can borrow his clothes and return them dirty.

If the tactics in stage one do not work you need to intensify your efforts. You must move from being annoying to being offensive. Such as getting a big, shaggy dog and letting it sleep on your roomates bed while he is gone. Or you can forget to give him phone messages from his girl friend, you can even ask her for a date. You can also borrow his car and use all the gas without filling it up.

If stage two does not get rid of him, you must now resort to drastic measures. Two sure fire strategies will finish him off. One is to leave a fake message to yourself on the answering machine. The message should be from a doctor and should go something like this: "Mr. Jones, I hate to inform you that the tests were positive. This disease is often fatal and highly contagious. You must see a specialist at once." If this does not work he is too insensitive to move on his own and you must move to the second strategie. Wait until he leaves for the weekend, put his belongings in the hall, and change the locks on your doors. Its hard to get a good roomate. You need to find someone you can get along with.

37f Exercise 2

Point out which of the following titles would be effective for the papers described.

1. "Running: A Form of Anorexia"
   a formal paper that examines obsessive running as an emotional problem
2. "The Inquisitive Eye"
   an informative paper about new equipment for amateur photographers
3. "Health Foods"
   an argument that a diet of "health foods" is no more nutritious than any sensible eating program
4. "How to Choose a Long-Distance Company"
   an informative guide comparing rates and services of long-distance telephone companies

5. "Confessions of a Fraidy Cat"
    an impression of the writer's first day in the first grade—the fears
    and trials

37f Exercise 3

Choose effective titles for the ineffective ones in Exercise 2.

37g (8) Exercise 4

Proofread the following paragraph. Look especially for

transposed letters
omitted letters
repeated letters
omitted words
repeated words
incorrect capital letters
incorrect punctuation or mechanics

In 1834, when Richard Henry Dana, Jr., was a a sophmore at
Harvard, he cauught measles and consequently suffered serious
eye trouble. Temporarilly unable to use his eyes, he became an ordinary seaman, aboard the *Pilgrim* on its cruise from Boston
around Cape Horn to California. In califorma, Dana spent a year
gathering animal hides. Then, he returned to Boston on the the
ship *Alert*, attended The Harvard law School, and began work on a
book based on the journal he had kept during thhe voyage. In 1840,
he graduated from law school and that same yaer published *Two
Years Before the mast*, a realistic account of the suffering and
grievances of ordinary seamen. According Dana, the books purpose was to present "the life of a common sailor at sea as it really
is—the light and the dark together.

Chapter 38

COMPOSITION-IN-PROGRESS

No exercises.

PART VI

Special Writing Projects

Chapter 39

ARGUMENT AND CRITICAL THINKING

39a Exercise 1

List 10 subjects that you might want to develop for an argument. First, think about each subject in the list and discard any that you cannot consider objectively and critically, without prejudice. Second, consider the remaining subjects and discard any that do not interest you sufficiently to warrant the necessary research. Here are a few subjects just to get you started thinking: drunk-driving laws, "politically correct" speech, computer literacy, foreign-language requirements, salaries of professional athletes, early marriage, women in combat, drug testing.

39b Exercise 2

Consider once again your final list of subjects from Exercise 1. For each subject, ask questions and look for conflicting relationships. Pick two or more of the subjects that seem most promising and try to generate some statements on two sides of the issue.

39c Exercise 3

In Exercise 2, you were asked to choose several subjects and generate statements on two sides of an issue. Look back over the pros and cons you generated for each subject. Then write two theses for each subject, one thesis based on the pros and one based on the cons.

39d Exercise 4

Explain what kind of evidence you would look for to support the following claims.

1. Children watch too much television.
2. Television preachers depend more on showmanship than on theology.
3. Both Aldous Huxley in *Brave New World* and George Orwell in *1984* warn of the loss of individual freedom.
4. In political campaigns, advertising should be controlled to make campaigning equable for all candidates.
5. The school year should be lengthened.
6. If soil is not controlled, successful agriculture is doomed.
7. Patients should assume some responsibility for their own treatments and not rely solely on doctors.
8. Some people treat their animals like children.
9. Many popular video games have violent or destructive themes.
10. The violent and destructive themes of many video games lead to antisocial behavior.

39e (1) Exercise 5

Which of the following statements are facts? Which are opinions? Which are opinions backed up by facts?

1. Some people have rejected supermarket fruits and vegetables and instead buy from organic farmers, health-food stores, and food co-ops.
2. Edgar Allan Poe's dark view of the world can be traced to his mother's early death.
3. Food commercials are a dieter's enemy. They try to make food look delicious, fun to eat, and healthful.
4. *The Great Escape* contains unrealistic touches. In it, Steve McQueen, accompanied by the dramatic strains of the music score, vaults barbedwire fences on his motorcycle.
5. Al Capp not only created the funny comic strip *Li'l Abner* but also wrote very humorous prose.
6. For the study of birds, the contributions of amateurs can be important. Amateurs can contribute to science by keeping

detailed field notes about their observations of such information as bird behavior, numbers seen, weather, and terrain.

7. After their 1944 assassination attempt failed to kill Hitler, Ervin von Witzleben and General Karl-Heinrich von Stulpnagel were executed.

8. In America, drinking water is not harmful; wells and reservoirs are either naturally clean or are clarified. Filters in homes are therefore unnecessary.

9. By one estimate, less than 10 percent of America's 85 million bicycle riders wear helmets.

10. Used cars can be risky buys. A fair price is uncertain; odometers can be doctored to hide the mileage; damage can be camouflaged with fresh paint and polish; and little can be done in case you buy a lemon.

39e (1) Exercise 6

Assess the accuracy of the following passages. Is the tone rational? Is bias present? Is there evidence of research?

1. Before the South seceded from the Union, William S. Barry became absorbed in the contemplation of the great question of disunion, whose rapid approach his sagacity foresaw; and as it rolled its huge proportions to the brow of the political horizon, he became more and more convinced that, though beast it might be, it was far preferable to that *monstrum horrendum, informe, ingens,* of Northern fanaticism, whose ravages threatened the destruction of every Southern interest and Southern right. Mr. Barry was not a disunionist *per se,* and had used his best endeavors to stay the storm, so long as he considered an effort to do so consistent with manhood and honor.

2. Sport fishing may be changing. People once felt compelled to return to dock with as many fish as the boat could hold. They never thought about the waters getting overharvested. Nowadays, a new phase may be developing. More and more people believe that a fish is too valuable to catch just once, that catch-and-release is essential if the resources of our waters are to be protected. Recently on a chartered trip, after a long struggle, a young boy pulled on board a large king mackerel. After the con-

gratulations, he said, "Hurry, we've got to throw it back before it suffers." No one suggested keeping the fish. No one suggested a victory photo. The thrill was in the catch and in seeing the fish swim vigorously away. Perhaps we are learning to conserve our marine resources.

3. The feminist movement has completely ruined American society. Feminists constantly spout accusations that everything demeans women. They have encouraged women to dress like men and to go to work and abandon their family responsibilities. Feminists complain that they have no equality, but in truth they have instead too much equality. They are now suffering stress, alcoholism, and even heart attacks. They have alienated men to the point that marriage and children will never be possible. They should look around and see the damage that the movement has caused before it's too late.

4. The available information reveals considerable variety in the way steroids are taken. Both the amount and kinds of drugs taken differ. In a study of the drugs taken by competitive bodybuilders from Kansas and Missouri, Tricker, O'Neill, and Cook (1989) discovered that individual use ranged from one to fifteen different types of steroids. Pope and Katz (1988) reported that doses vary; some athletes take as much as 100 times the amount called for when the drug is taken as a legitimate medicine. Many athletes also "stack" drugs, taking several at once—from two to as many as six—and they administer the drugs both orally and by injection (Gaines, 1991).

39e (2) Exercise 7

Identify the types of emotional appeals and diversions that appear in the following statements.

1. Do-gooders who oppose capital punishment should have to pay for the expense of keeping a prisoner on death row.
2. The government of South Africa has been accused of despotism, but the country has been more economically successful than other African nations.
3. There is nothing wrong with buying research papers. If it were wrong, there would be no established businesses providing this service.

4. William Faulkner was an alcoholic; therefore he cannot be included in a discussion of serious writers.

5. It is not fair to make food manufacturers list all the ingredients included in a product. Consumers do not understand all the items being listed anyway.

6. All books containing any references to illegal drug use must be removed from public school libraries because we must teach wholesome American values to our children.

7. Soap operas must have some redeeming qualities because their ratings are extremely high.

8. Lie-detector tests are reliable. That fact was published by a nationally known newspaper.

9. It is un-American to favor gun control.

10. You cannot totally trust the lawyer's motives in the antiobscenity case; his wife once posed for *Playboy.*

39e (3) Exercise 8

Which of the following statements are generalizations based on inadequate evidence?

1. Diets do not work because a survey showed that 200 people who lost weight on diets eventually gained the weight back.

2. Vitamin C does not help colds; I took 250 milligrams for a month and still got a cold.

3. I thought I was drinking Coca-Cola, but I was told the drink was Pepsi; the two drinks taste exactly alike.

4. To determine the speed of the computer printers, we measured the time necessary to print a 170-word letter. We performed the test on 12 printers—4 laser printers, 4 ink-jet printers, and 4 dot-matrix printers. The laser printer proved to be the fastest, even faster than the dot-matrix models in their draft mode.

5. Barley can lower your cholesterol levels. Scientists at the University of Wisconsin found that chickens fed a barley-based diet had cholesterol levels in their flesh that were 30 percent lower than chickens fed the usual corn-based diet.

6. According to a study which traced the smoking habits of 25,000 people over a period of 10 years, 75 percent of those who quit smoking relapsed within a year.

7. Shakespeare could not have been the author of the works attributed to him. The real author was well traveled and showed

detailed knowledge of Venice in *The Merchant of Venice.* During his life, Shakespeare never left England.

8.   Many people still believe that President Roosevelt knew beforehand about Japanese plans to attack Pearl Harbor. Yet no credible evidence has ever been discovered to support that claim.

39e (4) Exercise 9

The following statements make poor evidence because of the language. In each, determine whether the language is obscure, abstract, or ambiguous.

1.   His intelligence scores are low; therefore, he cannot be expected to make an intelligent career decision.

2.   If the Vietnam war had been fought fairly, America would have never lost.

3.   Americans have the right to free speech. Therefore, I can say whatever I think.

4.   Section 62e provides that a custodial account will be treated as a qualified trust if such custodial account would, except for the fact that it is not a trust, constitute a qualified trust and the custodian is a bank or other person who demonstrates that the manner in which the assets will be held will be consistent with the requirements.

5.   College is a meaningful experience. Students learn a lot in college that they wouldn't otherwise learn. Students who want meaning in their lives should attend college.

6.   Because of the economy, the company has been forced to make organizational changes. The chief executive has decided that an involuntary termination program will be needed to facilitate the corporate upturn. Some of the restructuring will involve involuntary separation, but the company plans to implement an enhanced separation policy whenever possible. The chief executive insists that the primary concern will be for the human resources of the company.

7.   Run-to-run controls assure the accuracy or completeness of information received by a program. For example, following validation, control totals of valid transactions by transaction type are developed by the program which validated the transactions. Control records are written at the end of the transaction file

containing the control totals by transaction type.

8. Today, technology has made our lives easier and healthier. People have the power and freedom to develop a better world. Without technological improvements, our world would be much slower.

39e (5) Exercise 10

Point out the fallacy or fallacies in each of the following statements.

1. Since the security of our country is at stake, the CIA must have the freedom to collect information in any way necessary.
2. The rhino population has been affected either by poaching or by human encroachment.
3. The unreasonable medical fees of today's doctors should be subject to consumer protection laws.
4. The dodo was a species of bird that lived on the island of Mauritius in the Indian Ocean. The dodo could not fly and therefore became extinct.
5. We can improve our school system by giving up compulsory education. Then those who do not want an education can stay away, and the money can be better spent on the diligent students who remain.
6. The poor are deprived of necessities because of the money we have spent on space exploration.
7. Professor Brown gave no A's in Economics 101 last semester, so that course must be too hard.
8. The railroad system should be abolished because it is inefficient.
9. When a car has mechanical problems, we get a new one. In the same way, we should replace an employee with physical problems.
10. NASA should stop sending vehicles into space because every time one goes up, we have bad weather.

39f Exercise 11

Propose two subjects that would lend themselves to the classical structure; two, to the discovery structure; and two, to the Rogerian structure. Formulate theses for any three of the subjects and work up rough outlines.

39g Exercise 12

1. What is the purpose and effect of the first paragraph?
2. Point out the evidence that supports the thesis.
3. Are there any concessions to the opposition?
4. Does the writer include refutation?
5. Does the writer use the classical, the discovery, or the Rogerian structure? Or does he use a combination?

Chapter 40

RESEARCH PAPERS IN PROGRESS

40a Exercise 1

The following scenarios describe some of the circumstances that affect decisions about subjects for research papers. Judge the appropriateness of each subject in light of the criteria discussed in 40a.

1. The writer plans a 10- to 20-page paper on the errors made by Hitler in World War II but finds a 288-page book entitled *Hitler's Mistakes.*
2. The writer is taking an introductory course in biology and plans to write a five- to ten-page paper on the recent findings about genetic diseases. The sources contain terms such as *phenylketonuria, factor VIII replacement,* and *adenosine deaminase deficiency.*
3. The writer has a rather good understanding of computers and wants to write a 20-page paper about the advantages of computer use.
4. Because the writer once played Juliet in Shakespeare's *Romeo and Juliet,* she wants to know more about other female roles. She plans to write a 20-page paper on women in Shakespeare's plays.
5. The writer has heard of water pollution in other states and wants to find out the extent of this problem in his. A search of the library turns up only three articles, and one of them is eleven years old.

40a–40b Exercise 2

Answer the following questions to get an idea of how the purpose of a paper is linked to its subject.

1. What question or mystery is associated with three of the following? If you do not know, check in an encyclopedia or some other library source.

   the death of John F. Kennedy
   the events at the Alamo
   the building of the pyramids
   the identity of the dark lady of Shakespeare's sonnets
   water on Mars
   the meaning of dreams
   the Bermuda Triangle

2. What position could you argue in a research paper on three of the following issues? If necessary, use an encyclopedia or some other library source for background.

   the best Union Civil War general
   the turning point of the Kennedy–Nixon presidential campaign of 1960
   the causes of criminal behavior
   astrology's reliability
   immigration to America
   the guilt of Alger Hiss
   the Nagasaki bomb

3. Assume you must write a 10- to 20-page paper interpreting a literary work. Which of the following subjects seem appropriate for such a paper?

   evil characters in Shakespeare's plays
   the organization of Faulkner's *Absalom! Absalom!*
   a comparison of style in two poems titled "The Fish"—one by Elizabeth Bishop and one by Marianne Moore
   Voltaire's philosophy
   the similarity between Eudora Welty's version of the assassination of Medgar Evers and the actual assassinatiion
   the meaning of the underwater exploration in Adrienne Rich's poem "Diving into the Wreck"
   Jane Austin's skills as a novelist

40c Exercise 3

Answer these questions about your library.

1. Where is the reference area?
2. Which numbering system does your library use?
3. Where are the encyclopedias?
4. Where are the general biographies?
5. Where are the atlases?
6. Where are the almanacs?
7. Is your library's catalog a single alphabetical file or are the subject, title, and author files separated?
8. Is the catalog computerized?
9. Where is the *Library of Congress: Subject Headings?*
10. Where are the microfilms?
11. Where is the *Readers' Guide to Periodical Literature?*
12. Where is the *New York Times Index?*
13. Where is the *Monthly Catalog of United States Government Publications?*
14. Where are the specialized indexes and abstracts?
15. Does your library provide a computer search of the indexes?

40c Exercise 4

By using the resources of your library, find answers to the following questions. List the sources you used to find the answers.

1. What is the largest state east of the Mississippi?
2. Who wrote *Old Possum's Book of Practical Cats?*
3. Whose pseudonym was Diedrick Knickerbocker?
4. Who is the only President buried in Washington, D.C.?
5. What are quarks and squarks?
6. What is an example of a Spoonerism?
7. Who was Laodamia?
8. Who won the men's and women's singles competition at Wimbledon in 1965?
9. What is the origin of the word *infantry?*
10. Who played the dwarf in the 1931 version of *Frankenstein?*

40 d Exercise 5

Pick one of the following subjects or choose a subject of your own. Do enough preliminary research to decide on a specific purpose: to answer a question, to argue a position, to interpret literature. Then gather a working bibliography.

Union spies during the Civil War
Edgar Allan Poe's detective stories
The nutritional value of the hot dog
Pershing's pursuit of Pancho Villa
Zombies: fact or fiction
The perfume industry
The death of Mountbatten
Nineteenth-century attitudes toward venereal disease
Voyager's pictures of Uranus
The authenticity of *Clan of the Cave Bear*
The death and resurrection of Sherlock Holmes
Computer chess champions
Symbolism in Hemingway's *The Old Man and the Sea*
The food of Classical Greece
Elizabethan attitudes toward the Moors
Bohemian Paris in the 1880s
The pirate utopia of Libertatia
Esperanto: a universal language
The flying machines of Paul MacCready
The meaning of Oedipus's self-blinding
The discoverers of penicillin
Computers in the movie industry
El Niño's effect on the weather
The condition of the bullet that killed President Kennedy

40f Exercise 6

Using the material from the bibliography you gathered for Exercise 5, write a working outline. Note any sections that seem to lack coverage in your sources, that seem to be getting out of control, or that need to be added or deleted.

40h Exercise 7

Paraphrase each of the following passages and give credit to the source within the paraphrase.

1. Throughout the Middle Ages, and even later, it was widely believed that London had once been inhabited by giants, a legend which derived from the massive bones which were occasionally unearthed in and around the City. Sometimes these finds were put on display in City churches: during the sixteenth century, for instance, St. Mary Aldermary exhibited a huge thigh-bone, "more than after the proportion of five shank bones of any man now living," together with a twelve-foot drawing of a Goliath-like figure to assist the ignorant public in the work of reconstruction. (Robert Gray, *A History of London*)

2. A marathon is any kind of endurance contest—running, dancing, bicycling, flagpole-sitting. It is named for the narrow valley in Greece where in 490 B.C. the Athenians, under Miltiades, pinned down superior Persian forces so that they could not use their cavalry, and proceeded to slaughter them. The Persians lost 6,400 men in the battle; the Greeks, 192. Miltiades, fearing that Athens might surrender to Persian attack by sea in ignorance of the victory at Marathon, dispatched Pheidippides, his fastest runner, to take home the good news. Though nearly exhausted, having already run to Sparta and back, Pheidippides raced twenty-some miles to Athens, gasped out "Rejoice—we conquer!" and fell dead. (Willard R. Espy, *Thou Improper, Thou Uncommon Noun*)

40i Exercise 8

Take notes on the following passage as directed below.

There are, in fact, many puzzling features concerning sunspots, which may be answered once the causes of magnetic fields on an astronomic scale are worked out. For instance, the number of sunspots on the solar surface wax and wane in an eleven and one half year cycle. This was first established in 1843 by the German astronomer Heinrich Samuel Schwabe, who studied the face of the sun almost daily for seventeen years. Furthermore, the spots appear only at certain latitudes, and these latitudes shift as the cycle progresses. The spots show a certain magnetic orientation that reverses itself in each new cycle. Why all this should be so is still unknown. (Isaac Asimov, *Guide to Science*)

1. Quote the first two sentences.
2. Quote the second sentence and the last three sentences. Paraphrase enough remaining information for the note to make sense.
3. Paraphrase the entire passage.
4. Paraphrase the first sentence but quote the expression "puzzling features."
5. Summarize the entire passage.

Chapter 41

RESEARCH PAPERS
AND DOCUMENTATION

No Exercises

Appendix A

SPELLING

SPb Exercise 1

In each word, identify the final or only vowel sound as long or short. If the vowel is long, think of a companion word with a short vowel; if the vowel is short, think of companion word with a long vowel.

EXAMPLE: *rob,* short; *robe,* long

1. din
2. note
3. cur
4. envelop
5. shine

6. cute
7. tot
8. hate
9. wine
10. fat

SPb Exercise 2

For each base word, an appropriate suffix is listed. Indicate whether to drop or retain the *e* on the base word when adding the suffix.

1. argue + ment
2. encourage + ing
3. survive + al
4. immense + ly
5. use + ful

6. remove + able
7. face + less
8. whine + ing
9. trace + able
10. courage + ous

SPb Exercise 3

Decide whether to double the last consonant when making the past tense and past participle (adding *-d* or *-ed*) and the present participle (adding *-ing*) of each verb.

1. dare
2. engage
3. gag
4. omit
5. smoke

6. embed
7. assume
8. hope
9. sum
10. bud

SPb Exercise 4

Combine the following words, prefixes, and suffixes.

1. ir + responsible
2. awful + ly
3. under + rate
4. mis + spell
5. jack + knife

6. non + negotiable
7. dis + satisfy
8. fatal + ly
9. lamp + post
10. en + noble

SPb Exercise 5

Which of the following correctly spelled words follow the rules in the "*i* before *e*" school rhyme and which do not?

1. piece
2. receipt
3. leisure
4. friend
5. financier

6. yield
7. rein
8. protein
9. vein
10. foreign

SPb Exercise 6

Correct the incorrectly spelled "cede" words in the following sentences.

1. I was asked to intersede with the parents on behalf of the child.
2. Weight on the pulley should not exseed 50 pounds.

3. His bouts of depression were usually preceeded by visits from his creditors.
4. If the caution light comes, do not procede any farther.
5. In 1832, South Carolina threatened to sesede from the Union because of the national tariff.

SPa–c Exercise 7

Correct any misspelled words in the following passages. When the spelling patterns will not solve the problem, consult a dictionary or the lists of frequently misspelled words.

1. Last month I applied for a credit card at a major department store. The application ask for information that was completly unecessary: my hieght, my wieght, my religous preferance, and outragous details of my personel life. I dutiful filed out all the information. When I received the card, imagine my surprize to find that my name was mispelled and my address was incorrect.

2. Whenever I vow to begin a regular exercise program, something happens to interfer with my plans. For example, last Sunday, the sun was shinning, the temperture was 75 degrees, and my midterm test were behind me. So I determined to improve my physicle condition. I dug out my sweat suit and joging shoes and set out for the track. But providance was all ready preparing to intervene. Half way to the track, I had a flat tire. By the time I had gotton the tire fixed, the sun was gone and my intrest in musel tone had vanished.

Appendix B

ENGLISH AS A SECOND LANGUAGE

ESLa Exercise 1

Fill in the blanks with modifiers to produce expanded noun phrases.

1. _____ dog
2. a _____ day
3. Sergio's _____ _____ car
4. the _____ _____ horses
5. _____ _____ music

ESLb Exercise 2

Which of the following are count nouns with plural forms?

1. gravel
2. information
3. runway
4. essay
5. furniture

6. produce
7. laboratory
8. floor
9. parrot
10. homework

ESLb Exercise 3

Which of the nouns in Exercise 2 can be preceded by *much* and which by *many*?

ESLc Exercise 4

In the following noun phrases, correct any errors in the use of determiners. In some cases, you should change the determiners. In other cases, you should insert or delete determiners. Some of the determiners are correct.

1. a worst dust storm of the year
2. an eggs in the basket
3. a fourth of the property
4. a fourth row from the stage
5. least important of the novels
6. a trip down the Amazon River
7. those book on shelf
8. the Argentina's largest city
9. my mother's garden
10. everyone the problem

ESLc Exercise 5

Correct any errors in the use of determiners in the following passage. Some determiners in the passage are correct.

Mile is unit of length. First used by the Romans, mile unit was 5,000 feet long and contained about 1,000 the paces. In fact, a term *mile* comes from *milia passuum,* the Latin words for "thousand paces." On land, unit is equal to the 5,280 feet; on water, unit is equal to about 6,076 feet.

ESLc Exercise 6

At each asterisk (*), insert *a/an* or *the* where appropriate. Use no article where appropriate.

When *Bill Moyers interviewed *Jonas Salk, *medical researcher who is credited with developing *polio vaccine, Moyers mentioned that *Salk had used *fascinating term to describe his life. Salk claimed that he had spent his life learning *immortal lesson in *scriptures of *nature.

ESLd Exercise 7

Supply an appropriate pre-determiner for each noun phrase below.

1. the noise
2. the number of cars
3. her serious problems
4. a motor
5. their money for scholarships
6. his sisters
7. these dinner dishes
8. the cereal

ESLe Exercise 8

Put the following groups of words in the appropriate order to make a noun phrase.

1. oblong, big, the, baskets, straw
2. Japanese, all of the, in the league, players, baseball
3. Aristide's, examinations, final, both of, tomorrow
4. green, small, by the entrance, ornamental, three, bushes, holly
5. least, the conference, this year, important

ESLf Exercise 9

Add post-noun modifiers to the following noun phrases. You may use single words, prepositional phrases, or adjective clauses.

1. the birds
2. all the newspapers
3. a birthday party
4. our vacation
5. the extinction
6. an ancient civilization
7. a gift
8. two new paintings
9. the gas grill
10. a nursery

ESLh Exercise 10

Supply the appropriate verb in the tense specified in parentheses.

1. Donna Kaye (past tense of *value*) Gerry as a friend.
2. They (past tense of *have*) already left when we arrived.
3. Ms. Yang (present tense of *analyze*) our data.
4. I (present tense of *organize*) my notes every night.
5. The expense (past tense of *be*) more than I could manage.

6. A huge tapestry (past tense *hang*) in the hall.
7. Some of the magazines (past tense of *be*) out of date.
8. Simone (past tense of *grow*) weary of the lecture.

ESLi Exercise 11

Construct sentences using modal auxiliaries to express the concepts listed.

1. ability
2. necessity
3. prediction
4. invitation

5. advisability
6. possibility
7. fact

ESLg-j Exercise 12

Correct errors in the active-voice verb phrases below. Be sure to fill the same number of positions as are already filled in each phrase.

1. Glaucia *may had been sleeping.*
2. My gold fish *has acting* sick all week.
3. In the past, he *has went* to Italy for spring break.
4. The *had see* the movie twice already.
5. Students *should signing up* in the administration building.
6. The walls *was* cherry wood.
7. The clock *ring* at 6:00 every morning.
8. Last winter, I *buy* a new overcoat.
9. My uncle *can fixes* your computer.
10. The strike *have continuing* for several months.

ESLk Exercise 13

Correct errors in the passive-voice verb phrases below. Be sure to fill the same number of positions as are already filled in each phrase.

1. Janice *was give* a grant to study abroad.
2. Labor advanced greatly after the wheel *be invented.*
3. The meat *should been cooked* thoroughly.
4. Your baggage *have be take* to the Lost-and-Found department.

ESLk Exercise 14

Construct 5 sentences using a passive-voice verb phrase.

ESLm Exercise 15

Identify the verb chains in the following sentences.

1. Will they agree to rezone the area?
2. We decided to invite her to speak at the conference.
3. The security guard noticed smoke coming from the lobby.
4. Please remember to finish posting the entries.
5. I do not recall asking you to tell me about your surgery.

ESLm Exercise 16

Construct 10 sentences using chains of verbs.

ESLn–o Exercise 17

Make each positive statement below into (a) a negative and (b) a question.

1. The news was good.
2. An inquiry was held after the incident.
3. The girls had hidden in the closet.
4. Lightening struck the fire tower.
5. The opera opens tomorrow night.
6. An employee will be available to collect tickets.
7. All the students finished the quiz on time.
8. We have been looking for a good programmer.

ESLp Exercise 18

Use the tag-question test to determine which of the following words groups are complete sentences.

1. People allergic to dairy products should take calcium supplements.

2. Most plants reproduce by pollination.
3. Cultivating rice with water standing on the fields.
4. Diego Rivera's murals in the National Palace in Mexico City.
5. The area was not secured properly.
6. She lived on campus and ate in the cafeteria.
7. The paper not a good quality.
8. Both husband and wife must list their assets.
9. After the tide went out.
10. Because a driver's license is required to cash a check.
11. Charles decided to work on his master's degree at Arizona State.
12. Not using a cheap outdoor paint.

ESLp Exercise 19

Rewrite the sentence fragments in Exercise 18 as complete sentences.